Research in Criminology

Series Editors
Alfred Blumstein
David P. Farrington

Research in Criminology

continued after index

A.D. Biderman
J.P. Lynch

Understanding Crime Incidence Statistics

Why the UCR Diverges From the NCS

With Contributions by James L. Peterson

With 11 Figures

Springer-Verlag
New York Berlin Heidelberg London Paris
Tokyo Hong Kong Barcelona Budapest

Albert D. Biderman
Department of Justice, Law, and Society, The American University, Washington, DC 20016, USA.

James P. Lynch
Department of Justice, Law, and Society, The American University, Washington, DC 20016, USA.

Contributor
James L. Peterson
Child Trends, Inc., 2100 M Street, Washington, DC 20036, USA.

Series Editors
Alfred Blumstein
School of Urban and Public Affairs, Carnegie-Mellon University, Pittsburgh, PA 15213, USA.

David P. Farrington
Institute of Criminology, University of Cambridge, Cambridge, CB3 9DT, UK.

Library of Congress Cataloging-in-Publication Data
Biderman, Albert D.
    Understanding crime incidence statistics: why the UCR diverges
from the NCS/Albert D. Biderman, James P. Lynch.
        p.   cm.—(Research in criminology)
    Bibliography: p.
    Includes index.
    ISBN 0-387-97045-2
    1. Criminal statistics—United States—Evaluation.   2. National
crime survey report.   3. Uniform crime reports (Washington, D.C.)
I. Lynch, James P. (James Patrick), 1949–   . II. Title.
III. Series
HV6787.B53   1989
364′.042′015195—dc20   89-11576

Printed on acid-free paper.

Typeset by Best-Set Typesetter Ltd., Hong Kong.
Printed and bound by Braun-Brumfield, Ann Arbor, MI.
Printed in the United States of America.

9 8 7 6 5 4 3 2 1

ISBN 0-387-97045-2 Springer-Verlag New York Berlin Heidelberg
ISBN 3-540-97045-2 Springer-Verlag Berlin Heidelberg New York

Acknowledgments

This research was funded in part by the Bureau of Justice Statistics of the Department of Justice under Contracts J-LEAA-015-79 and J-JSIA-004-82. Some of the data utilized in this paper were made available by the Inter-University Consortium for Political and Social Research (ICPSR). The data from the National Crime Surveys were originally collected by the Law Enforcement Assistance Administration (now the Bureau of Justice Statistics). Neither the Bureau of Justice Statistics nor the Consortium bears any responsibility for the analyses or interpretations presented here.

The authors would like to thank Albert J. Reiss, Jr., David Cantor, and Yoshio Akayama for comments on earlier drafts of the papers that constitute this volume. We would also like to acknowledge the contributions of Elizabeth Jabine, Beah Zander, Norma Chapman, and Janie Funkhauser, formerly of the Bureau of Social Science Research, Inc., as well as Paul Zolbe, former Director of the Federal Bureau of Investigation's Uniform Crime Reports section, Ken Kendall of the UCR staff, and Al Paez, Robert Tinari, and Larry McGinn of the U.S. Bureau of the Census. Mona Danner of The American University deserves special recognition for her assistance in updating the analyses presented in the original papers. We would like to thank Al Blumstein for encouraging us to update and combine our original papers into this monograph. Finally, thanks are due to Carolyn and Alex for their patience.

Contents

Introduction

The prominence achieved by the novel measure of "households touched by crime" when it was introduced into the National Crime Survey (NCS) in 1981 was responsible for renewed attention to comparisons between the crime rates reported by the NCS and the Uniform Crime Reports (UCR). The new NCS measure suggested that crime was declining; this at a time of widespread awareness that the UCR Index was at all-time highs. Comparisons of the NCS and UCR in *The New York Times* (1981) and the *Washington Post* (1981) had the unfortunate consequence of reviving old and usually ill-informed arguments about which is the "better" measure of "trends in crime." More recent discrepant changes of the two measures in 1986 and 1987 rekindled the debate, although with somewhat diminished stridency.

The efforts of criminological statisticians to develop an appreciation for the two statistical systems as quite different but complementary measures have suffered a setback in these debates, but an opportunity is also afforded to improve the understanding of crime statistics by officials, the media, and the public. The need remains for the Bureau of Justice Statistics (BJS), the Federal Bureau of Investigation (FBI), and the research community to explain in quantitative terms the ways in which the two systems attend to different, albeit overlapping, aspects of the crime problem. The two systems use methods that differ in their strengths and weaknesses, and employ quite different kinds of indexes to summarize the parts of the crime problem they do measure. To be sure, improvements can be made in both systems so that such discrepancies as occur are due more exclusively to divergent changes in the crime problem encompassed by each system's measures.

NCS and UCR will regularly encounter "Let's you and him fight!" provocations. It is extremely important for the future of both the UCR and the NCS, as well as for the intelligent and effective use of their products, that they are provoked only to enhance the light each system can shed on the other and to increase the capacity of each system as a useful and accurate measure of crime problems. The systems have become truly complementary. NCS is only viable so long as there is some other system that is unaffected by its limited scope of crimes and small-sample limitations. UCR will always have to confront the question from its users, "Well, how about unreported crime and changes in reporting?" And, at least until the UCR does something to separate offenses against private persons and households from those against businesses, and to provide other illuminating disaggregations of its data, such users as criminologists, the vigorous victim-advocacy movement, and the press will be looking elsewhere for their data.

For some time, it has been important to spell out reasons why the NCS and UCR rates could move in divergent directions, particularly for reasons having nothing to do with their error properties. Although it has been pointed out on a number of occasions that such discrepancy could take place, it is now clear that we were remiss in not predicting that it would take place. Such discrepancies, as we will suggest below, have been predictable for some time.

This monograph examines the issue of discrepancy. We identify factors that could cause the two series to move in opposite directions and estimate the relative importance of these factors using series data. This effort differs in several ways from previous attempts to "reconcile" the two series (Cohen and Land, 1984; Cohen and Lichbach, 1982; Decker, Shichor, and O'Brien, 1982; O'Brien, 1985; Nelson, 1978; Skogan, 1974). First, it examines the trends or changes in the two series and not the cross-sectional relationships between them across places. The NCS and the UCR are primarily used as indicators of the change in level of crime nationally, and therefore, understanding of discrepancies with respect to annual change estimates is of utmost importance. Second, we used panel data from the NCS to address the issue of discrepancy, rather than data from one-time or episodic surveys collected in specific cities. It is unclear exactly how applicable findings from one-time surveys in one jurisdiction are to the NCS Panel. Third, our intention is to understand why the two series diverge, not to get them to track more closely. Reconciliation assumes that NCS and UCR annual rates should change similarly. This predisposition encourages the examination of those factors that will make the trends track, while ignoring influences that cause them to diverge. Moreover, reconciliation as a goal can encourage the acceptance of adjustments that produce the desired result, but offer no conceptual explanation for why they should. Such an approach reconciles the two series, but does not contribute to our understanding of discrepancy. Fourth, we approach this study with the assumption that differences in the definitions and procedures of large-scale statistical systems can have large and systematic effects on the consistency of their trends. These effects may be direct or by interaction with changes in the society. Consequently, we give more attention to procedural differences between the systems than previous studies of the two series did.

Chapter 1 presents some basic descriptive information on the NCS and the UCR that will be helpful in understanding the discussions in subsequent chapters. Most of this information pertains to the two series during the period 1973 through 1986. Some attention is given to the extensive evaluations of the series that occurred throughout the 1980s and the subsequent changes that are expected in each in the early 1990s.

Chapter 2 examines the time series of the UCR Index and the NCS for the years 1973 to 1986 (the entire period for which NCS public-use tapes were available when this book was begun) to assess the extent to which the impression of discrepancy arises from differences in (1) the scope of crimes each series is designed to cover, (2) the procedural differences in their construction of the crime events, which form the numerators of their published rates, and (3) the different population counts each series uses for rate denominators. This analysis examines these definitional and procedural differences between the two statistical systems as potential sources of the discrepancy in time series, rather than the inadequacies of implementation or other sources of measurement error. Demographic and other social changes during the years in question are considered that may affect the two series differently. Some attention is given to the implications of the planned changes in the systems for the exploration of discrepancy in the 1990s.

This book's focus is on change in the aggregate, "Total Crime" indexes because that is the focus of the most prominent and influential uses to which these series are put. The search for a valid aggregate indicator of the "level of crime" in the nation gave impetus to both series, and it remains a major basis of their political support. The institutionalization of the NCS appears to have helped gain broader media attention to differentiated statistics of crime, but the original NCS design mimicked the UCR's single-number index emphasis. That our focus on aggregates greatly simplifies our examination of the two systems is an incidental result. Crime-specific topics have been largely relegated to an appendix (Appendix A).

Chapter 3 examines the contributions of nonuniformities in measurement in the NCS and UCR to the differences in the time series. Some of the discrepancy in the series is due to the nonuniform application of definitions and procedures or to changes in procedures that facilitate data collection but affect the measurement of a phenomenon that each purports to measure. For example, when UCR participants report two burglaries in a motel as separate incidents rather than as one, they have misapplied the "hotel" rule and have introduced nonuniformity of the former type. When the Census chooses to include data from unbounded interviews in making NCS estimates, the estimates will be higher than if the same respondents were given bounded interview treatment. When such effects systematically occur and affect the series in contradictory ways over time, then they contribute to discrepancy. In Chapter 3 we begin to explore the contribution of measurement variability to discrepancy, using information on measurement effects in the NCS. We specify the direction and magnitude of effects on aggregate-rate estimates of some variable aspects of procedures, in both the NCS and the UCR, that are known to have consequential effects. Simple adjustments are made in the series for major sources of measurement variability, and these adjusted series are compared to assess their importance for discrepancies between the two series.

Chapter 4 summarizes the major findings of the previous chapters and presents some conclusions about the principal sources of discrepancy, about the information and analyses required to further our understanding of discrepancy, and about changes in both systems that would increase the light that each sheds on the crime problem.

1
Describing the Uniform Crime Reports and the National Crime Survey

Much of the discussion that follows assumes some knowledge of the organization and procedures of the Uniform Crime Reports (UCR) and the National Crime Survey (NCS). For readers not familiar with these data collection systems, this chapter provides a brief description of each. The origin and history of each system are reviewed. We describe the organization of the systems as well as the procedures used to collect the data. Special attention is given to recent changes in each series that could affect series comparisons and to substantial redesigns that both systems have undergone.

The Uniform Crime Reporting System[1]

Recognizing the need for a national crime statistics program, the International Association of Chiefs of Police (IACP) developed the Uniform Crime Reporting Program. IACP surveyed local police agencies to obtain data on crimes known to and recorded by the police. Because not all types of crime are equally well reported to the police, the Chiefs decided to focus on seven types of crime that were (1) prevalent, (2) serious, and (3) well reported to the police (FBI, 1985a). These seven types of crime included homicide, rape, robbery, aggravated assault, burglary, larceny, and motor-vehicle theft. Participants in the UCR report all of these seven types of index crime or Part I offenses coming to their attention. The reporting of other offenses (Part II offenses) is not mandatory. Arrests made in both Part I and Part II categories were to be reported, as well as data on law-enforcement personnel.

---

[1] This discussion of the Uniform Crime Reports relies heavily on excerpts from *Study of the National Uniform Crime Reporting Program of the Federal Bureau of Investigation: Phase I Interim Report*. Eugene Poggio et al., Cambridge, MA, Abt Associates, December 1983.

The IACP transferred responsibility for the UCR to DOJ in July 1930, and the FBI began publishing the UCR in September of that year.

The UCR program changed little from 1930 to 1958, aside from the slow but steady growth in the number of police departments participating. The information content and organization of the system remained formally essentially that outlined by the IACP. In 1958 a number of changes were made in the system (Poggio et al. 1983). The Crime Index was used in UCR reports. Negligent manslaughter and larceny under $50 were eliminated from Part I crimes, but continued to be reported as Part II crimes. Statutory rape was eliminated entirely. Intercensal population estimates were used rather than estimates from the previous decennial census.[2] Quarterly summary reports were initiated.

After these changes, the formal organization and content of the UCR system changed in no major way until the early 1970s.[3] At that time the Law Enforcement Assistance Administration (LEAA) encouraged the development of UCR state programs by providing start-up funds. More than 42 states have programs. These programs serve as intermediaries between the local police departments and the FBI. They provide technical assistance and training to police personnel within the state. They also collect and classify data from the jurisdictions and send the information to the federal UCR program. In addition, the legislation creating state programs also mandated reporting by law-enforcement agencies within the states. The introduction of state programs almost doubled the number of agencies reporting to the UCR.[4]

Organization of the Current UCR Program

The organization of data collection and dissemination in the UCR depends to a large extent on whether there is a state program and whether reporting is incident or summary based. In jurisdictions with a state program, local police departments report to that program which in turn forwards these reports to the Federal Bureau of Investigation (FBI). In

---

[2] Although intercensal estimates are more accurate than the last decennial census data, even these estimates become progressively less accurate as the decade progresses. More will be said about this in subsequent chapters.

[3] There have been numerous small changes and supplementations of the system from 1958 on. These changes included the introduction of a Supplementary Homicide Report, finer distinctions within the robbery category according to the type of weapon used, the return to including all larcenies regardless of amount of loss, and the addition of arson to Part I crimes (but not the Crime Index). For a useful summary of these changes see Poggio et al., 1983, Table 2.2.

[4] It should be noted, however, that the percentage of the U.S. population covered by the UCR increased by only 6%. Even viewed in these terms, however, the increase in coverage was substantial.

other states the local police department sends its data directly to the FBI. Incident-based systems report data on each individual crime known to the police. Each burglary, for example, would be the subject of an incident report that is sent to the state program or the FBI. In summary systems, the local agencies simply report counts of crimes known to the police. The states not having state programs are direct summary systems in which crime counts are reported directly to the FBI. A few states with state programs are incident-based reporting systems, most states have summary-based systems, and several have mixed systems in which some agencies report incident data and others report summary data[5] (Poggio et al., 1983).

Data Elements

The UCR system collects data on all crimes except traffic offenses and federal crimes. The offenses are grouped into two categories: Part I and Part II. Counts of the number of offenses reported to the police, as well as arrest and clearance rates, are collected for Part I offenses, whereas only arrest data are reported for Part II offenses. The Part I offenses include criminal homicide, forcible rape, robbery, aggravated assault, burglary, larceny-theft, motor-vehicle theft, and, since 1978, arson. All other offenses are categorized as Part II offenses. For the purposes of the Uniform Crime Reports, offenses are reported by a uniform definition rather than by a state's own penal code.

For the Part I offenses, UCR collects information on all offenses known or reported to the police, regardless of whether an arrest resulted. In addition to the number of offenses reported or known, data are collected on the number of these reports proved to be unfounded (false or baseless), the number of offenses cleared by arrest or exceptional means, and the number of clearances involving only persons under 18. The monetary value of property stolen and recovered is recorded for Part I offenses. Also, details relevant to specific Part I offenses are collected, for example, weapon, offender, and victim characteristics, and circumstances of murders; the type of weapon and type of premise in robberies; and the time and premise type (residential or nonresidential) of burglaries.

Information on arrests is collected for both Part I and Part II offenses, including information on the offender's age, sex, race, and ethnic origin. For juveniles, arrest information includes data on police disposition, that is, whether the offender was handled within the department and released or referred to a court or other agency.

Finally, the UCR collects information on law-enforcement personnel. It collects data on officers killed and assaulted and conducts a yearly

---

[5] For a state-by-state description of the organization or the UCR see Poggio et al., 1983, Table 3.2.

count of law-enforcement employees by department. Employees are distinguished according to their sworn or civilian status, full- or part-time status and their sex.

Classifying and Scoring

Classifying is determining the proper crime categories by which to report offenses in UCR; scoring is counting the number of offenses after they have been classified and entering the total count on the appropriate UCR reporting form.[6] The principal classification and scoring rules can be briefly described:

1. *The Hierarchy Rule.* In situations where several crimes are committed simultaneously, the Hierarchy Rule requires classifying each offense, determining which are Part I offenses, using a ranking list that ranges from murder down to motor-vehicle theft, and then deciding which is the highest-ranking offense. That offense alone is scored; the other offenses involved in the incident are ignored.[7] The Hierarchy Rule applies to all index offenses except arson, which, if committed in conjunction with another index offense, is counted in addition to that offense.

2. *Crimes Against Persons Versus Crimes Against Property.* For crimes against persons—criminal homicide, forcible rape, and aggravated assault—UCR scores one offense for each victim. Thus, if four men rape three women, three offenses are counted. Crimes against property are robbery, burglary, larceny-theft, motor-vehicle theft, and arson. For these crimes, UCR scores one offense for each distinct operation. Thus, if a robber in a tavern orders five people to hand over their wallets, only one offense is counted.

3. *The Hotel Rule.* This rule further defines the "distinct operations" counted for crimes against property. The Hotel Rule applies to "burglaries of hotels, motels, lodging houses, and other places where lodging of transients is the main purpose. . . . If a number of dwelling units or commercial spaces under a single manager are burglarized and the offenses are most likely to be reported to the police by the manager rather than the individual tenants, the burglary should be scored as one offense."[8] Thus, although the Hotel Rule applies to hotels, it does not apply to apartment buildings, office buildings, rental storage units, or other similar structures.

4. *Jurisdictional Guidelines.* Jurisdictional guidelines are aimed at preventing agencies with overlapping jurisdictions from double-counting the same event. Police report offenses that occur within their city's

---

[6] FBI, *UCR Handbook*, 1982, p. 33.
[7] *Ibid.*
[8] *Ibid.*, p. 20.

jurisdiction; county and state law-enforcement agencies report offenses occurring in the county outside the jurisdiction of the city. More than one agency may respond to the same criminal event, yet for UCR purposes, the event should be scored only once, by the agency in whose jurisdiction the event occurred.

Reporting Requirements

Thirty states have statutes that mandate law-enforcement-agency reporting. Often the legislation does not specify participation in the UCR program per se, but rather requires that law-enforcement departments submit crime data as designated by a state agency, for example, the state police or state attorney general's office. It is, then, a state agency that decides whether to collect information according to UCR criteria. Fifteen of the statutes specify penalties for noncompliance. These penalties include fines, jail terms, withdrawing state funds from the department, removing the top administrator for malfeasance, withholding the salary of the individual responsible for reporting, and punishment as determined by the state's attorney general.

Every state program and the FBI require contributors to submit UCR data at least once each month, even if there has been no activity in a jurisdiction. Generally, both summary-based departments and automated incident-based departments follow a monthly reporting schedule, although some incident-based departments that report on paper forms send data more frequently.

The monthly submission includes seven forms: the Return of Offenses Known to the Police (Return A); Supplement to Return A; Juvenile Age, Sex, Race, and Ethnic Origin (ASREO) Report; Adult ASREO Report; Report of Law Enforcement Officers Killed or Assaulted (LEOKA); Supplementary Homicide Report; and Report of Arson Offenses Known to the Police.

Quality Control Procedures

The extent of quality-control procedures utilized at both the state and local levels varies considerably. The variety of checks by local contributors ranges from no review in a summary-based department where one police officer has been designated the UCR expert, to a sophisticated dual reporting system in which calls for service are entered into both an automated records system and a manual log. Officers dictate their reports, including narratives, via telephone to clerks, who enter them into the automated system and then into the manual log to indicate their receipt. Copies of the reports are simultaneously reviewed by patrol sergeants and coded for UCR by a records clerk. Finally, the reports are forwarded to a special UCR review section that checks suspect reports.

There are a number of other review mechanisms in place. Local contributors whose UCR operations are automated rely on programmed edit checks to identify errors. These systems work two ways: (1) They prevent certain incorrect data elements from being entered by refusing to accept the information; and (2) they find and denote on reports mathematical mistakes, logical inconsistencies, and missing information.[9] Most automated departments verify keypunched data, that is, information is keypunched twice with the two entries being compared for errors made during data entry.

All state programs perform edit checks of the data submitted to them by local reporting entities. Manual edits include visual reviews for completeness and reasonableness of the data, cross-checking totals among forms, arithmetic tallies to validate additions, and statistical verification when crime trends show large fluctuations. Automated edit checks search for logical inconsistencies in the data, omission of information, duplicate reporting, arithmetic errors, and discrepancies in data across reports.

Generally, when a state program receives hardcopy data from local contributors, the forms are reviewed by the state's field liaison for that agency or by staff designated specifically to perform this quality-control function. If the state program then reports to the FBI via computer tape, corrected forms are sent to a data-processing unit for keypunching or direct entry into an automated system. It is at this point that programmed edit checks are applied.

For those local departments that submit computer tapes to their state programs, the state's visual inspections occur after the tapes have been printed. At this point, the computer has flagged errors or potential errors in the data, either on a separate error listing or on a master printout of all the data.

The Crime Statistics Processing Unit of the FBI-UCR section is responsible for data entry and quality control of the statistics contributed both by state programs and agencies that report directly to the FBI. Processing of hardcopy data-reporting forms includes recording receipt of the documents, editing them prior to data entry, entering the data, and filing the documents. When the forms are received, they are checked to ensure that nothing is missing and that each contributor's forms are grouped together. Receipt of each form is recorded on an agency checklist, which can be used to ascertain whether data are available and whether an agency is a regular contributor. Once the forms have been stamped and recorded, they are examined to see if the agency identifiers and month codes are correct and to check the reasonableness of the offense counts and monetary values. Some of the other edits conducted at this point include

---

[9] The former type of automated edit check is possible only with on-line data entry, whereas the latter is possible with either on-line entry or batch processing.

comparing the number of arrests on the ASREO report with the number of clearances on the Return A to see if they are compatible;[10] comparing the total number of law-enforcement officers killed or assaulted as listed on the Return A with the LEOKA form to see if they match; comparing the number of murders on the Return A with the number of victims on the Supplementary Homicide Report to see if they are the same; and comparing property values to see if the grand totals match the totals of the breakdowns, for larceny and auto theft, for example.

After this review, the data are entered into the minicomputer, verified, and edited. These edit checks include addition, Return A offense counts versus Supplement offense counts, excessive amounts, and others. Afterwards, the data are transferred to magnetic tape and the corresponding UCR master files are updated.

When the FBI receives UCR reports on computer tape from a state program, they log them in and transfer the data to an FBI magnetic tape. A copy sheet is generated listing record counts for each type of report and each month. From this point, processing the computer printout listings closely follows the steps used with the paper forms (described above) with the exception of the third step, entering the data.

The effectiveness of these data-control techniques varies by type of system and data problem. They are particularly good at identifying errors in computation as well as keypunching and some coding errors. They are less well suited for detecting falsification, omissions of descriptive information in the original report, and misclassification of incidents due to incomplete or erroneous information on the original offense report. Only full-scale audits could provide such information routinely. The effectiveness of the edits and other quality controls currently employed can be greater in incident-based systems than in summary systems. Inappropriate values in reports and logical inconsistencies apparent in a single incident will not be identifiable in aggregated tallies. The practice of editing only returns that depart from expectation and, furthermore, may have biased the series toward these expectations (Biderman, 1966:111–129).

Corrective Action

Local UCR reporting entities take corrective action when their own review process indicates that amendments are needed, and when state or FBI program personnel direct them to do so. The changes may be as simple as reading a column of numbers or as complicated as locating a victim to obtain a property value or asking an officer to supply a critical element of information that was left out of a report. The Abt survey of

---

[10] There is no standard definition of compatibility. According to interviews conducted as part of the Abt study (1983), comparability means whatever is reasonable in the judgment of the person responsible for quality control.

UCR programs and local police departments suggests that there is no typical approach or level of commitment to corrective actions across places or data problems (Poggio et al., 1983).

State UCR program personnel responsible for rectifying problematic reports include field coordinators, trainers, audit/support staff, and even program directors themselves. According to responses received in Abt's survey of state UCR programs, most states attempt to correct contributors' reports on their own, if possible, or via telephone contact with the local agency.

When errors are serious or indicative of a pattern, field representatives make personal visits to the department to explain the problem and assist with the corrections. Remedial training may also be scheduled. One state reported that if errors involve misunderstandings of policies or procedures, they are reviewed and discussed in the state's UCR newsletter.

Reports

Routine reports are provided by the state programs on a monthly, quarterly, or annual basis to local contributors. Every state program publishes an annual report. Only a few send monthly and quarterly reports to program participants. The Abt survey (Poggio et al., 1983) found that all of the states visited collected and reported back to the contributors data beyond that required by the UCR program. In most cases this reporting involves a crime or set of crimes of particular interest to state or local authorities.

The FBI distributes UCR data in a number of reports and, more recently, in machine-readable form through the Inter-University Consortium for Political and Social Research (ICPSR). *Crime in the United States* is the principal FBI publication. It is released annually in August or September. It presents information on Part I offenses and arrests as well as Part II arrest data and information on law-enforcement personnel. There is an official midyear release as well as a preliminary annual report that appears in the late spring. Three special reports are produced annually: *Bomb Summary*, *Assaults on Federal Officers*, and *Law Enforcement Officers Killed*.

In addition to these routine publications both the FBI and the state programs prepare special reports and data tapes upon request.

The Redesigned UCR

In the early 1980s, the law-enforcement community called for a thorough evaluation of the UCR with the objective of recommending a revised program to meet law enforcement needs into the 21st century. The FBI formulated a three-phase redesign effort and Bureau of Justice Statistics (BJS) underwrote the first two phases in which Abt Associates recommended the changes to be made in the current program. The third phase involved implementation of the recommended changes (FBI, 1988a).

In the first phase, Abt documented the current system. All aspects of the program including its objectives, intended audiences, data content, reporting procedures, quality controls, publications, and user services were examined. The second phase was devoted to examining alternative formats for the redesigned UCR. This phase ended in 1985 with the production of the draft *Blueprint for the Future of the Uniform Crime Reporting Program* (BJS, 1985).

The *Blueprint* called for a radical revision of the current UCR program. The program would move from summary to incident-based reporting. It would also involve two tiers. One would be similar in content to the existing program (but incident based) and include all agencies participating in the current program. The second tier, Level II, would include much more extensive information than presently required and would involve all agencies serving populations of over 100,000 and a sample of jurisdictions under 100,000. The additional information available in Level II would include type of victim, victim characteristics, victim-offender relationship, use of force or weapon, type and nature of injury, time, type of location and residence status of victim. The proposed system would also permit, at both levels, multiple offenses rather than mutually exclusive classification based on the hierarchy rule and the linkage of arrest and offense records. The Abt study also called for substantial enhancement of the UCR's quality-assurance program, including the conduct of routine audits (BJS, 1985).

The third phase of the redesign calls for the implementation of the recommendations contained in the *Blueprint*. Several significant steps have been taken in the implementation process, (FBI, 1988d). New offense definitions have been developed and new data elements defined (e.g., offender characteristics, weapon types). These definitions and procedures were tested in one state program. On the basis of this pretest, three volumes have been prepared describing the system and its implementation for use by interested jurisdictions (FBI, 1988b,c,d).

One major change in the implementation process has occurred since the *Blueprint* and that is the abandonment of the two-tiered system. It appears that most reporting jurisdictions will immediately opt for the implementation of the Level II system (FBI, 1988a). This decision may have the unfortunate consequence of delaying the availability of nationally representative incident-based data on offenses known to the police. If jurisdictions are allowed to go to full implementation as they choose, rather than on the basis of a probability sample, then a nationally representative system will not be in place until virtually all jurisdictions are ready to operate with the sophistication that Level II requires.[11] On the other hand, the fiscal and political limitations on implementation may be such that piecemeal implementation is the only alternative.

The FBI estimates that the full implementation of the system will "be a long enterprise" (FBI, 1988d). There were no published timetables for implementation or usable information on the number of systems ready to move to full implementation. There were some indications, however, that incident-level UCR information for a number of states might be available as early as 1991.[12] Approximately 12 states were expected to provide test data for the incident-level system by the end of 1989. Another dozen states were expected to report this data by 1990. A large number of states are reporting implementation activity (BJS, 1989). All of this suggests that, while complete implementation in the population of law enforcement agencies may be "a long enterprise," some incident-level data will be available in short order.

The National Crime Survey

The National Crime Survey (NCS) collects data on personal and household victimization through an ongoing national survey of residential addresses. The survey was designed to achieve four primary objectives: to develop detailed information about the victims and consequences of crime, to estimate the numbers and types of crime not reported to the police, to provide uniform measures of selected types of crimes, and to permit comparisons over time and types of areas. The survey provides measures for the following types of crimes, including attempts: rape, robbery,

---

[11] It is possible to draw a representative sample of agencies independently of the implementation process. Jurisdictions would implement the incident-based system as they could. A sample of jurisdictions could be drawn that would be representative of the population of police agencies. Some of these sample agencies would be in jurisdictions that have implemented the incident system and some would not. The data for agencies with incident-based systems could be used to impute information for agencies that had not implemented the new UCR systems. This approach to providing nationally representative data for the new UCR may be feasible. It rests, however, on the tenuous assumption that agencies in jurisdictions that have implemented the incident-based system are similar to agencies that have not in all important respects. If this approach to providing national estimates before full implementation is chosen, then this assumption must be thoroughly examined. Extensive work in imputation models must be done. More importantly, studies of agencies in jurisdictions that have implemented the system and of agencies in those that have not must be conducted to ensure that they are the same in all important respects.

[12] This information was provided by Paul White of the Bureau of Justice Statistics in a personal communication on March 8, 1989.

assault (including both simple and aggravated), burglary, larceny, and auto or motor-vehicle theft. Detailed information about each victimization incident is recorded as well as the characteristics of the offender insofar as the victim can report them.

The original design of NCS consisted of surveys of both households and commercial establishments, nationally and in selected American cities. Collection of data for commercial establishments and in specific cities ended in 1975, and in 1977 for the national sample. Only the national sample data collection continues and this does not include commercial crimes.

The NCS traces its immediate origins to the work performed for the President's Commission on Law Enforcement and the Administration of Justice, impaneled in 1965. One important issue that the commission considered was the need for accurate information on the amount and distribution of crime. Traditionally, such information was limited to official statistics on the activities of law-enforcement agencies or the judiciary. These figures had long been criticized as representing only a small fraction of the events occurring in society that might be characterized as criminal. Significant problems were seen in the reliance upon official statistics of crimes known both because many events are not reported to police and many other organizational and administrative influences may affect particular jurisdictions and their reports.

By the 1960s, the methodology of sample surveys was sufficiently developed to allow exploration of ways in which they might be applied to the problem of measuring crime. Such surveys were seen as a means whereby new measurements of crime were possible. Survey-based measures could serve as a social indicator of the incidence of crime and provide detailed information on the characteristics and circumstances of events that were defined as criminal. Such information would allow the examination of a wide variety of important topics, including who was victimized by different types of crimes and how often, the consequences of victimization in injury and financial loss, the willingness of victims to report crimes to the police, and the characteristics of offenders as reported by victims. It was also believed that accurate and timely estimates of the incidence of crime could be developed to allow comparisons over time and assess statistics available from official sources, especially the UCR counts of crimes known to the police.

Several field surveys were conducted for the President's Commission and revealed both that statistics on crimes known to the police underrepresented the amount of crime and that the measurement of victimization with sample surveys was feasible, though for many reasons difficult (Biderman et al., 1967; Ennis, 1967; Reiss, 1967). The following were among the problems of self-report surveys of victimization as these were seen at the time by the investigators who were conducting the methodological research for design of the NCS:

1. *Choice of reference period.* Respondents have varying ability to recall victimization experiences. This variation was seen to be dependent in part upon the length of the reference period for which the respondent was asked to recall incidents. The longer the period the less complete the recall. If the NCS was to estimate the incidence of victimization for specific time periods, it was important to determine the reference period that would elicit the most reliable results, given reasonable limits on the frequency with which the surveys could be conducted.

2. *Temporal displacement.* In retrospective surveys respondents tend to report incidents as occurring later or earlier than they did. This displacement can cause errors in estimating victimization for a given period of time. Some method had to be found to minimize temporal displacement.

3. *Asking about household property.* Some property that is the target of theft belongs to households rather than individuals. It may be possible to obtain accurate reporting of thefts of household property by asking only one member of the household about such thefts. If this is the case, then accurate information could be obtained from one respondent rather than asking all household members. If one household respondent could not report accurately on the theft of household property, then all members must be interviewed. This, however, would increase costs and raise the problem of identifying and eliminating duplicate information.

4. *Accommodating incapable or unavailable respondents.* Some portion of the population cannot be interviewed because they cannot speak the language, are incompetent or considered incompetent, or they are consistently unavailable. It is important to include the experience of these populations in a victimization survey. Methods had to be found to include the victimization of these populations within acceptable cost limits.

Other issues of methodological importance included questionnaire design, especially the screen questions (designed to elicit reports of victimization), respondent selection, the order of administration of instruments, and the classification of incidents. Skogan and Lehnen (1981) reviewed BJS measurement issues in victimization surveys.

A substantial amount of research was done on the appropriate methodology to use in addressing these design problems. Based in part upon this research, the BJS, in consultation with the Census Bureau, adopted a rotating panel design of a sample of addresses in the United States. Housing units were retained in sample for a 3½-year period during which interviewers return to a housing unit every 6 months to conduct interviews with the current residents of the unit. This 6-month reference period was thought to be the best trade-off between accuracy of recall, sample size, and interview frequency. The data obtained the first time a unit is in sample is not used to estimate victimization rates. The purpose was to control temporal displacement by conducting this prior interview. Subsequent interviews at the housing unit were used on the theory that the previous interview bounds the subsequent interview. All household members are asked about their experience with personal crime, but only one member is asked to report on crimes involving theft or attempted theft of household property. The experience of respondents who cannot speak English or Spanish or are otherwise unable to be interviewed is obtained from a proxy (usually the household head). All 12- and 13-year-old household members were interviewed by proxy.

Each respondent is asked a series of screen questions to determine if he or she was victimized during the 6-month period preceding the first day of the month of interview. Seven screen questions concern crimes assumed to affect all occupants of a household so are asked of one member. They deal with break-ins or attempts, thefts at or near the home and thefts of motor vehicles and motor-vehicle parts. Although all household members are not asked these screen questions, a household incident will still be recorded if it is mentioned by a secondary respondent. Another 13 screen questions, asked of all respondents, concern specific types of personal crimes, other incidents reported to the police, or any events the respondents thought might be a crime. Whenever a respondent makes a positive reply to a screen question, he or she is asked "how many times" that type of incident occurred during the reference period. At the conclusion of the screen questions, an individual victimization report is completed for each incident mentioned in response to the screen questions.

This basic design has been used since inception of the survey in 1973. Although the design has remained the same, other changes have been made in the size of the sample, the number of questions, and the mode of interviewing. In order to reduce costs, the size of the NCS sample was cut in June 1984 from 72,000 to 59,000. The proportion of interviews conducted by telephone rather than in person has increased throughout the life of the survey. A substantial increase in the telephone component of the interviewing took place between 1979, when 80% of the interviewing was by personal visit, and 1980, when roughly equal numbers of interviews were being done in person and by telephone. In order to reduce costs, the proportion of telephone interviews has steadily increased since 1980, to the point where 80% of all interviews in 1988 were being done by done on the phone.

A number of changes were made in the questionnaire in 1979.[13]

Sample Design and Size

Originally, the National Sample consisted of approximately 72,000 sample housing units selected in a stratified multistage cluster sample from the

---

[13] For a more extensive discussion of changes in the NCS, see Martin, 1983.

1921 Primary Sampling Units (PSUs) formed with counties or groups of counties using every county in the U.S. The PSUs were grouped into strata by combining PSUs with similar characteristics into 220 strata and allocating a single self-representing PSU to the remaining 156 strata. The first stage of the sampling procedure consisted of the selection of an interviewing site from each of the strata. Beyond the 156 PSUs selected with certainty, a single PSU per stratum was selected with a probability proportionate to size in the 220 combined strata. Beginning in June 1984, a sample cut resulted in the reduction of the 220 non-self-representing (NSR) strata to a group of size 153. This also included a 20% sample reduction in the larger of the 156 self-representing (SR) PSUs. Even with this smaller number of sample areas, the reliability of estimates has been maintained by using crime-related characteristics in the formation of the strata and by improving sample selection with the PSUs.

The sample of housing units within a PSU was selected in two stages. In the first stage, Enumeration Districts (EDs)[14] were systematically selected with a probability proportionate to their 1970 or 1980 population size from a geographically arranged listing. In the second stage, each previously selected ED was subdivided into segments of about four housing units from which a sample of segments was then selected.[15]

The current National Sample of 59,000 housing units yields approximately 40,000 interviewed households in the 50 states and the District of Columbia for a 6-month period. Because of the continuing nature of the National Sample Survey, a rotation scheme was devised to avoid interviewing the same household indefinitely in order to avoid poor cooperation or biased responses resulting from repeated interviewing. The sample of housing units is divided into six rotation groups with each group being interviewed every 6 months for 3½ years.

Within each rotation group six panels are designated, with a different panel interviewed each month during the 6-month period. The first interview for a housing unit in a group is used only for bounding and is not included in the regular public-use data. However, if a new household moves into a sample unit, the members of that household are interviewed and their unbounded interviews are included in the data. Thus, the number of incident reports associated with a household may be affected by its tenure in the sample.

---

[14] Enumeration Districts are geographic areas ranging in size from a city block to several hundred square miles, usually encompassing from 750 to 1,500 persons, established for the 1970 and 1980 Censuses of Population and Housing.

[15] Whenever possible, the segments were formed from the list of addresses compiled during the 1970 or 1980 Censuses. Housing units built after the 1970 or 1980 Census were sampled primarily from lists of new construction units. Since data from the 1980 Decennial have become available, they have been employed in adjusting weights and in revising the current sample design.

TABLE 1.1. NCS rotation group structure.

Interview month	First sample						Second sample (rotation)					
	1	2	3	4	5	6	1	2	3	4	5	6
January	1	1	1	1	1	1	(1)ᵃ					
February	2	2	2	2	2	2	(2)					
March	3	3	3	3	3	3	(3)					
April	4	4	4	4	4	4	(4)					
May	5	5	5	5	5	5	(5)					
June	6	6	6	6	6	6	(6)					
July		1	1	1	1	1	1	(1)				
August		2	2	2	2	2	2	(2)				
September		3	3	3	3	3	3	(3)				
October		4	4	4	4	4	4	(4)				
November		5	5	5	5	5	5	(5)				
December		6	6	6	6	6	6	(6)				
January			1	1	1	1	1	1	(1)			
February			2	2	2	2	2	2	(2)			
March			3	3	3	3	3	3	(3)			
April			4	4	4	4	4	4	(4)			
May			5	5	5	5	5	5	(5)			
June			6	6	6	6	6	6	(6)			
July				1	1	1	1	1	1	(1)		
August				2	2	2	2	2	2	(2)		
September				3	3	3	3	3	3	(3)		
October				4	4	4	4	4	4	(4)		
November				5	5	5	5	5	5	(5)		
December				6	6	6	6	6	6	(6)		
January					1	1	1	1	1	1	(1)	
February					2	2	2	2	2	2	(2)	
March					3	3	3	3	3	3	(3)	
April					4	4	4	4	4	4	(4)	
May					5	5	5	5	5	5	(5)	
June					6	6	6	6	6	6	(6)	
July						1	1	1	1	1	1	(1)
August						2	2	2	2	2	2	(2)
September						3	3	3	3	3	3	(3)
October						4	4	4	4	4	4	(4)
November						5	5	5	5	5	5	(5)
December						6	6	6	6	6	6	(6)

ᵃ Numbers in parenthesis indicate panels that are being interviewed for the first time.

Table 1.1 is an illustration of the NCS rotation scheme across three hypothetical interview years. Two complete samples with six rotation groups are shown as one sample is rotated out and the other is rotated in. In the body of the table, the panel number within each group is shown opposite the month(s) in which they are interviewed for the first time. The results of these interviews will be used for bounding only and will not appear in the data file used to generate victimization estimates.

Data Collection

The Questionnaire Forms

Three basic forms are used to collect the required data for the NCS—the Control Card, the Basic Screen Questionnaire, and the Crime-Incident Report. A number of changes have been made over time in the NCS instruments and the procedures for administering them, and some of these are noted in the documentation. A more comprehensive and detailed description of these changes is available in Martin (1983).

The Control Card is the basic administrative record for each sample unit. It contains the address of each sample unit and the basic household data, such as the names of all persons living there and their age, race, sex, marital status, education and the like. Family income, tenure of the unit, and pertinent information about noninterviews are also included on the Control Card. The Control Card serves as a record of visits, telephone calls, interviews, and noninterview reasons. The Control-Card information is updated, as needed, during each visit to the housing unit except questions about educational attainment, family income, and tenure, which are only asked every other visit.

The Basic Screen Questionnaires are used to record characteristics of all household members 12 years of age and older in a sample unit, as well as to screen for incidents of crime that were committed against the household and/or household members. Information about the general characteristics of the household and each household member are transcribed by the interviewer from the Control Card. Household and individual Screen Questionnaires are designed to elicit information on whether any crimes were committed against the household as a whole or specifically against individual household members. Respondents may on occasion volunteer reports of household incidents not mentioned by the household respondent or victimizations of another household member that the victim failed to mention. In such cases the interviewer fills in an incident report by interviewing the appropriate person.

A Crime-Incident Report is used to gather the detailed information about crimes reported in either the Household or Individual Screen Questions. One Crime-Incident Report is completed for each incident of crime reported in answer to screen questions. For example, if a respondent said that his pocket was picked once and he was beaten up twice, three Crime-Incident Reports, one for each separate incident, are completed. Under certain circumstances interviewers are allowed to report several incidents as a "series" on one Incident Report form. The following conditions must be met before a series incident is reported:

1. Incidents must be of the same type or very similar in detail.
2. There must be at least three incidents in the series.

3. The respondent must not be able to recall dates and other details of the individual incidents well enough to have reported them separately.

Interviewers are instructed to try through probing to get individual reports whenever possible and only accept series reports as a last resort. If a series incident report is made, the questions apply to the most recent occurrence within the reference period.

Interviewing

Prior to an interview visit, each sample unit is sent a letter from the Bureau of the Census informing the household about the National Crime Survey. During each enumeration period, initial interviews are conducted with as many household members as possible during a personal visit. Questions pertaining to the entire household are asked only once. These questions are answered by a single household respondent who could reasonably be expected to know the answers pertaining to the household. Individual Screen Questions on the Basic Questionnaires are asked as many times as there are household members age 12 and older. Information about each household member 14 years and older is obtained by a self-response; however, information about members 12 and 13 years old is obtained by proxy from either the household respondent or some other knowledgeable household member.[16] The average face-to-face household interview lasts 30 minutes. Subsequent interviews may be conducted by telephone if it is more efficient or less costly. The Bureau of the Census has made greater use of telephone interviewing in recent years as a cost-saving measure. Beginning in February 1980, telephone interviews were done during the second, fourth, and sixth interviews for households that had access to a phone, and where the household respondent indicated to the interviewer that a telephone interview was acceptable. Beginning in March 1986, telephone interviews were conducted for all interview periods except for the first and fifth interview period.

A sample unit for which an interview could not be obtained is classified as one of four noninterview types. Type A noninterviews consist of households occupied by persons eligible for interviews but from whom no interviews were obtained because, for example, no one was found at home in spite of repeated visits or because no occupant was willing to be interviewed. Because Type A noninterviews are considered avoidable, every effort is made to convert them to interviews. Type B noninterviews are for units that are unoccupied or that are occupied solely by persons who have a usual residence elsewhere (URE). Type C noninterviews are units ineligible for the sample because the unit is demolished, condemned, or no address was listed. Type Z noninterviews occur when an interviewer

---

[16] In July 1986 self-report as opposed to proxy interviews were begun with 12- and 13-year-olds whenever possible.

is unable to obtain an interview for a particular household member in an otherwise interviewed household.

Interviewer instructions are explicit and detailed concerning the administration of the questionnaires, adherence to question wording, and the use of probes. Only the questions are read, not the response categories. Interviewers are instructed to read response categories only as a last resort. They are explicitly instructed to avoid reading the answer categories for the question, "How were you threatened?" if at all possible. Thus, for instance, respondents are not asked directly if they were raped or threatened with rape; they must volunteer the information in response to questions about how they were attacked or threatened. Residue is used in the codebook documentation to designate those cases where the respondent could not or did not provide an answer, or for some reason the response given did not fall into the predetermined categories.

Quality Control

Interviewers receive extensive training prior to any field work. The quality of interviewing is maintained by periodic direct observation of all interviewers, office edits of completed work, and verification of their work by reinterviewing a sample of completed sample units.

Reinterviews measure how well individual interviewers followed procedures. They also measure errors in coverage of the population resulting from missing units, incorrect address listing, and so forth. The reinterview procedure is used to evaluate the impact of errors or variations in responses.

Reporting of NCS Data

NCS data are provided in publications and in machine-readable form through the Inter-University Consortium on Political and Social Research (ICPSR). BJS issues several annual reports using NCS data including *Criminal Victimization in the United States*, preliminary and final change reports, and the bulletin *Households Touched by Crime*. In addition to these annual publications, NCS data have been analyzed for a variety of special reports dealing with specific types of crime (e.g., stranger to stranger crime, rape, household burglary, family violence), crimes against special populations (the elderly, teenage victims, Hispanics), and with specific features of crimes (weapons use, costs of crime).[17] NCS data are also routinely made available in various compendia including the *Report to the Nation on Crime and Justice*, the *Sourcebook of Criminal Justice Statistics*, and the annual *Statistical Abstract of the United States*.

---

[17] For a more complete listing of these publications, see the back flap of any issue of *Criminal Victimization in the United States*, 1987, p. 121, or call BJS.

Machine-readable NCS data are made available through ICPSR. These files are updated annually and include both complete files of NCS data (both victims and nonvictims) and extract files containing only victims and crime incidents. These files are provided in hierarchical and rectangular formats. Other special-purpose data files developed from NCS data for special reports are also available for public use.

The National Crime Survey Redesign[18]

The redesign of the NCS began when congressional interest in the survey prompted LEAA to commission an evaluation of the program by the National Academy of Sciences (NAS). The Academy's recommendations were published in 1976 (Pennick and Owens, 1976). Following the evaluation an internal review of the survey program by LEAA staff was begun. A conference was held in 1978 to discuss topics and priorities for a 5-year program of research that would address issues raised by the NAS evaluation. This conference and a related utilization study indicated a need for an extensive examination and possible redesign of the NCS. A Request for Proposal was issued in 1978 and a contract awarded to the Bureau of Social Science Research, Inc. (BSSR), in 1979. BSSR organized a consortium of experts in criminology, survey design, and statistics that reexamined all aspects of the survey including questionnaire design, sample, collection strategies, administration, error properties, dissemination, and utilization of the data. The variety of topics that had to be addressed in the redesign required a consortium format because no one organization could be expected to have experts in all facets of survey design and utilization.[19]

The redesign proceeded in three phases. The first was devoted to identifying all of the immediate improvements that could be made in the survey and to organize the investigation of these improvements. The second phase emphasized the development of near-term changes in the survey that could improve the NCS without incurring large costs or disrupting the data series. These recommendations could be implemented almost immediately. The third phase addressed more fundamental changes in the survey that would substantially increase the quality of the data or reduce costs. It was understood that these changes may be costly to implement and could disrupt the series unless some splicing strategy was

---

[18] Much of this section is excerpted from Taylor (1989).

[19] The following organizations participated in the Crime Survey Redesign Consortium (CRSC) at one time or another: (1) Carnegie-Mellon University, (2) National Opinion Research Center, (3) Research Triangle Institute, (4) Survey Research Center, University of Michigan, (5) Westat, Inc., (6) Yale University.

employed. The introduction of these changes would require substantial lead time and could only be implemented over the long term.

Within each of these phases, the work of the consortium proceeded in an iterative fashion. Potential improvements were suggested. Arguments were made regarding the desirability of the proposal and the information necessary to evaluate it was obtained. Very often this process involved design work (e.g., developing survey instruments and small-scale testing) in order to determine whether a particular proposal was feasible. When the information was assembled, a decision was made about recommending the proposed improvement to BJS. Proposals that survived this process were recommended to BJS and supporting documentation was provided.

In 1983, the CSRC proposed a set of recommendations for implementation in the near-term. These included:

Screening and Scope Changes

1. *Including vandalism in the NCS.* Vandalism is a highly prevalent crime that exacts a tremendous cost on individuals and society. No other data system currently includes this offense.
2. *Interviewing 12- and 13-year-olds directly and not by proxy.* Proxy interviewing results in the under reporting of victimization incidents. Although this does not radically affect overall rates, it does substantially affect rates for juveniles.

Expanding Incident Descriptions

3. *Revising place of occurrence codes.* Current location codes do not permit consistent distinctions regarding the publicness of places or their exposure. Moreover, it is impossible to identify crimes occurring in the respondent's neighborhood. Changes should be made to permit these important distinctions.
4. *Adding codes to identify crimes occurring in the respondent's town.* It is important to be able to identify crimes that occur in the town of residence versus those that happen elsewhere. All of the geographic data in the survey can be used with the former but not with the latter. Also, for future comparisons with the UCR, allocating victimizations to place of occurrence (rather than residence) is crucial.
5. *Obtaining information on victim–offender interaction.* The common wisdom on crime prevention is replete with prescriptions for situational responses to victimization. There is no systematic data that can be used to test this wisdom.
6. *Expanding information on the outcomes of victimization incidents.* Although we have information on the loss or injury resulting from victimization events, we have little data on the response of the criminal justice and other systems to crime. More information should be obtained on the nature of the service received by victims after the incident.

Increasing Explanatory Variables

7. *Fielding routine supplements to the NCS that can be used to distinguish victims from nonvictims.* The core NCS instrument has remained constant because of potential effects on annual rate estimates. This constancy has limited the extent to which the NCS can be used to increase our understanding of victimization risk. Introduce controlled variation in the content of the NCS with supplements administered to portions of the sample. This will provide the variation necessary for explanatory models without disrupting the series.

8. *Collecting more information on perceived motivation of offenders including the role of substance abuse.*

Changing Crime Classification and Reporting

9. *Using collection-period data for estimation purposes.* Given the NCS design data on a particular reference year are not available until 9 months after the end of that year. This time lag could be reduced if preliminary estimates based on collection year data were used.

10. *Adjusting annual rate estimates for major sources of measurement error.* Nonuniformities in measurement can affect changes in rates. Models should be developed to adjust for known sources of error in annual rate and change estimates.

11. *Increasing the power of statistical tests used in the NCS through the use of empirical variances.* The time series of the NCS is long enough to be used to derive empirical variances for annual estimates. These variances may be quite different from the theoretically derived estimates currently used to assess the reliability of year-to-year change.

Of these recommendations BJS accepted the direct interviewing of 12- and 13-year-olds, the use of periodic supplements, the expansion of victim behavior information in the incident form, expansion of questioning on victim lifestyles, revision of the place of occurrence codes, changes to the codes describing weapons use, expanding information on outcomes of victimization, production of state-and county-level tapes, and use of collection-year estimates. The scope of crimes covered in the survey was not expanded to include vandalism because BJS and Census felt that such a change would disrupt the series. The implementation of this change was deferred to the long term. The use of error-adjustment models and empirical variances was accepted in principle, but more development work was necessary by the Census Bureau before such practices could be introduced. This development work would be done as the production work of the survey permitted.

The recommendations accepted by BJS were introduced into the survey in July 1986 following a period of design work and field testing by the Census Bureau.

In 1985, the CSRC recommended to BJS changes to be implemented over the long term. These recommendations focused on seven major aspects of the survey design that would have substantial implications for the cost of the survey or the quality of the resulting data.

Quality Enhancements

1. *Make the NCS a longitudinal survey of persons.* The NCS interviewers return to housing units every 6 months for 3½ years, but the occupants of these units change. A design that followed persons would simplify estimation (no unbounded interviews) and offer analytical opportunities (e.g., establishing temporal order) that the current design does not.
2. *Use a 4-month rather than a 6-month reference period.* A shorter reference period would reduce underreporting of victimization events.
3. *Use interview-to-interview recounting rather than recounting to the beginning of the month in which the interview is conducted.* Using the first day of the interview month as the near bound of the reference period needlessly complicates the recall task and encourages temporal displacement of events reported. Using the interview as the near bound would simplify the recall task and thereby reduce underreporting of victimization.
4. *Employ more productive short-cue screeners to encourage more complete reporting of victimization.* Field tests demonstrated that a short cue screening interview can provide more cues per unit time than more syntactically complex approaches. This, in turn, promotes more complete reporting of victimization events.
5. *Use centralized telephone interviews.* Centralized telephone interviewing enhances control over interviewers, thereby ensuring more reliable data.

Cost-Reducing Changes

6. *Maximize the use of telephone interviewing.* Telephone interviews are less expensive to conduct than in-person interviews and there is no convincing evidence that they provide less accurate information.
7. *Use data from the bounding interview for estimation purposes.* One-sixth of the interviews conducted in the NCS are not used for estimation purposes. Adjustment models can be applied to these bounding interviews and they can be used to produce annual estimates. This will increase the effective sample size of the survey or permit sample reductions with no loss in precision.

Because the adoption of a particular feature has implications for the feasibility or desirability of the others, these design components were combined into total design packages. It was generally agreed that two of

TABLE 1.2. Design packages considered for implementation over the long term.

Design package	Longitudinal design	4-month reference period	Central telephone	Maximum telephone	Use of bonding Interview
1	X				
2	X			X	X
3	X		X	X	X
4	X	X	X	X	X
5		X	X	X	X
6			X	X	X

the design components—interview-to-interview recounting and the use of the short-cue screener—were desirable features of any recommended design. The nature of the design ultimately recommended would therefore turn on the other six design features. Dual-frame sample designs were rejected because of the Census's bad experience with cold-contact telephone interviewing. This left five design components for consideration. Although all possible design packages were considered, six more promising alternatives were considered at length. These six designs are presented in Table 1.2.

Of these six design packages, number 3 and number 6 were recommended to BJS for implementation over the long term. BJS accepted design package number 3 for implementation in the long term.

The implementation of some of the long term changes in the survey will proceed at a different pace from others. Tests of the short-cues screener and a revised incident form have been completed and the new instruments are being phased into the NCS. Phase-in was to take until 1992. Centralized telephone interviewing will be phased in at the same time as the new instrumentation. Interview-to-interview recounting has been introduced. Implementation of the longitudinal design was delayed to await the review of the Survey of Income and Program Participation (SIPP) longitudinal processing system. Such a processing system is essential for a longitudinal survey and BJS cannot afford to do the development work required for such a system. Borrowing from the SIPP experience will substantially reduce these development costs. If the SIPP experience is successful, then a true longitudinal design may be implemented in the NCS.[20] Census is in the process of developing models for the adjustment of bounding interviews. This work will be complete by the phase-in of the new instrumentation.

---

[20] BJS has proposed an interim step in which a supplement to the NCS will be used to follow a subset of vitims. Although this approach will provide data on the enduring outcomes of victimization, it will not yield the information necessary for exploring factors affecting victimization risk.

Conclusion

The NCS and the UCR are radically different in their organization and procedures. Unfortunately, there is a widespread perception that the two systems measure the same phenomena in similar ways. Given this perspective, it is incumbent upon us in the crime-statistics community to describe how these organizational and procedural differences could cause the trends to diverge without either series being in error. Subsequent chapters will address this issue. Most of the analysis will pertain to the period 1973 through 1986, although some attention will be given to the implications of the NCS and UCR redesigns for the study of divergence.

2
Why the NCS and the UCR Crime Index Appear Discrepant as Indicators of Trends in Crime

The correct but imprecise belief that the NCS and the UCR measure trends in crime has helped foster the impressions of discrepancies between the two series. Given that both systems measure "Crime," the expectation is that the two series should track each other over time. In fact, the NCS and UCR attend by design to two different, although overlapping, sets of crime events. Naive comparisons of trends in the two series often have failed to identify the components of the crime problem common to both and therefore involved comparisons of the incomparable. Consequently, impressions of discrepancy have been created where no consequential inconsistency existed.

Apparent discrepancies also arose from differences in the procedures used to classify and count incidents in the two systems. Even the timing of BJS and the FBI releases have unwittingly contributed to the perception that the two trends have moved in different directions.

This chapter reviews the differences in scope, definitions, and procedures in the NCS and the UCR that could contribute to the appearance of discrepancy between the series. Whenever possible, we adjust the series to estimate the single and combined contributions of these factors to their having yielded at times divergent impressions of the change in the rate of incidence of crime.

NCS Reporting Lags and False Impressions

Before treating the contribution of procedural and definitional differences to the discrepancy of the two indicators of change in crime, we will consider one important factor that helped foster a widespread impression that the NCS has consistently presented a rosier picture of change than did the UCR.

In the recent past—1979 to 1982—people's impressions of a discrepancy between NCS and UCR trends were accentuated by the coincidence of the period of years immediately following the founding of the NCS with an

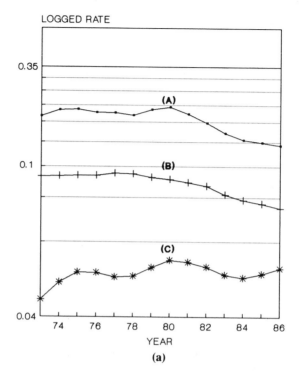

LOGGED RATE

(a)

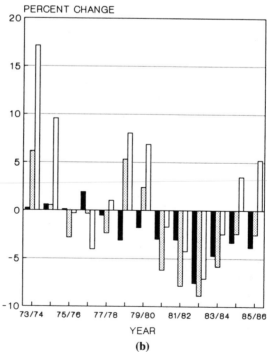

PERCENT CHANGE

(b)

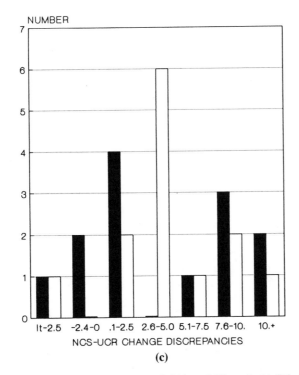

NUMBER

NCS-UCR CHANGE DISCREPANCIES

(c)

FIGURE 2.1. (a) The official NCS Personal (A) and Household (B) Crime Rates are substantially greater than UCR Index (C) Crime Rates. (b) Annual percent changes in the UCR Index Rates (white bars) were larger than the NCS Personal (black) and Household (dotted) changes in the 1970s and occasionally in opposite directions. Changes in NCS Household Rates exceed those of the UCR in the 1980s. (c) Differences between the annual percent change in the NCS Household Rates and percent change of the UCR Index (white bar) were usually small, while the differences between changes in the UCR and NCS Personal Crime Rate (black bar) were larger and more variable.

unusual pattern of changes in the UCR Index. The mid-1970s departed from the pattern of the immediately preceding period in that the UCR Index did not show constant increases. Indeed, for most of the offense categories, there was a 2-year or 3-year period of falling rates beginning about 1975 and no increase in the UCR total Index during the period 1975 to 1977 (see Figure 2.1). The string of consistent increases in the UCR rates occurred at the very end of the decade. Prior to 1979, the UCR and NCS rate changes would not have appeared discordant. But the lag in producing NCS series precluded people from making comparisons immediately during the period when the series were moving in the same direction. The lag in reporting NCS data was then much greater than it was for the UCR. The result was that people were reading a headline based on the UCR proclaiming that crime was going up soon after being exposed to another story based on the NCS proclaiming that it wasn't. As a determinant of impressions, the particular statistical reference period on which a "current" indicator is based can be less important than its release date. Without realizing it or without giving it sufficient attention, journalists early in the eighties were implicitly juxtaposing impressions they derived from NCS releases covering 1973 to 1978 with the very sharp increases in the UCR that occurred after 1978.

The following excerpt from *Newsweek* (1981) illustrates the problems posed by reporting lags:

Is America caught in another crime wave? The answer depends on where you look. The standard statistical measure is the FBI Uniform Crime Reports, a compilation of offenses reported to the police. In 1979, after resting several years at a high plateau, the rates of reported crime edged forward. But in 1980 they exploded. . . . And across the nation the figures for the first six months of 1980 showed a 10 percent jump in serious crime. . . .

Another measure of crime—some experts believe a better one—is the census bureau's semiannual survey of victims. Unlike police reports, the victimization studies are not subject to police manipulation and do not rely on a 911 telephone emergency system that is different in every city. Between 1973 and 1979 the sampling of victims shows no signs of a surge.

Emphasis is given to the most recent FBI data for 1980, while the NCS data cited pertain to the period 1979 and earlier.

Recent changes in the release of NCS annual estimates of the level and change in crime seem to have eliminated this source of misperception. Since 1982, the NCS has been issuing an indicator of the prevalence of crime—households touched by crime—9 months after the end of the reference year in contrast to the 18-month lag that was typical for the period prior to 1982. These NCS releases in August or September are essentially coincident with the FBI's release date for *Crime in the United States*. Moreover, by accepting the CSRC's recommendation that collection period data be used for publishable preliminary estimates, BJS has been able to release annual estimates of level and change in crime at approximately the same time that the FBI issues its preliminary estimates, that is, in March or April. With these changes in the dissemination of the NCS data, it should be possible to issue a joint release including both NCS and UCR estimates of change in crime.

Comparing Statistics From Samples and Nonsamples

Another factor making for discordant impressions of the two series has been the sample-survey character of the NCS. Even with its large sample size and even for most aggregated yearly change indicators, the NCS has limited statistical power. An observed difference from one year to the next in victimization rates must be fairly substantial for it to be accepted by BJS with the statistical confidence permitting it to say that an actual change in a particular direction has taken place. For example, the NCS must show approximately a 3 to 4 percent change in aggregate rates before the BJS will announce with confidence that the crime rate has changed. Much larger changes must be observed for less prevalent crime classes such as rape (47.8% change) or robbery (18.4% change). The conventional sampling rhetoric used by BJS and the Census Bureau being what it is, statements of their uncertainty regarding whether a change actually took place often are readily misinterpretable by the press and public as very scientific assertions that no change took place. For instance, a recent BJS Bulletin, declared:

Rates for the three household crimes measured by the NCS—burglary, household larceny, and motor vehicle theft—remained basically unchanged between 1985 and 1986 (BJS, 1986:2).

In the associated table, asterisks next to the values for the percentage change in rates for each of these types of crime refer to the footnote:

*The difference is *not* statistically significant at the 90% confidence level (BJS, 1986:3).

The 1985 to 1986 "basically unchanged" household larceny observation, however, represented a continuation of a sharp, uninterrupted downward trend of that rate that had persisted for a decade and that had totaled 30% during that period. The 1985 to 1986 change exceeded the average change for the years in question.

Because the NCS is a sample, confidence intervals are computed to account for the error that sampling could introduce. No comparable device exists for the UCR Total Crime Index for attempting to take into account how much it may depart from the value that would have been obtained if it were actually based on complete data from every last one of the police jurisdictions in the US.

Not quite all agencies do report their data. The agencies reporting known Index offenses to the FBI include jurisdictions covering between 95% and 98% of the U.S. population in a given year. Although the excluded jurisdictions are only a small proportion of the total, their exclusion introduces some unknown amount of error. Also, the FBI has often excluded from a given year's Index data for jurisdictions, including some of the nation's largest, which it regarded as suspect.

A broader problem is posed by the fact that a substantial proportion of the participating police departments fail to report for all 12 months of the year. This is equivalent to nonresponse in surveys.

The UCR and the NCS both use imputation, where they feel it warranted, to incorporate values for missing data into their indexes. The imputation methods are discussed further in Chapter 3. The UCR differs from the NCS, however, in that its published reports do not indicate how or how much imputation is involved in its Index. Nor does it provide statistical estimates of the magnitudes of deviations from the values that would have resulted were various data not missing, as the Census Bureau does by attending to nonresponse in forming its variance estimates for the NCS.

Whenever comparisons are made between the two series, the BJS must give some attention to the sampling error of the NCS. Changes in NCS rates are evaluated in order to estimate the probability that the observed change could be due to sampling error. Only where this test leads to the conclusion that a change as large as that observed is unlikely to have been due to sampling error does BJS note the change. Because year-to-year changes in both systems are quite small, on average, the computation of standard errors and the choice of confidence interval in the NCS can be quite consequential for perceptions of divergence. When both the NCS and the UCR show a slight increase, but the increase in the NCS is not statistically significant, the FBI announces an increase and BJS says no significant change took place. This was the case, for example, between 1986 and 1987. In this instance, use of a smaller standard error and confidence interval might have led to announcements of increases in both trends and the perception of convergence.

It is possible that the method for computing the standard error of estimates in the NCS may be more conservative than it need be. Indeed, evidence to that effect can be found in published NCS estimates. We examined the differences in property crime rates across age, race and sex groups that we had good reason to believe would not change overtime, so that any change in these differences would probably be due to sampling error. Specifically, we computed the difference in crime rates between persons 50 to 64 years of age and persons 65 and older for race (white/nonwhite) and sex groups in each year from 1973 to 1986. In all, 56 differences were examined. Given the sample size and variability in crime rates in the NCS, the expectation is that sampling variability alone would yield 5 or 6 "significant" differences among the 56 comparisons of group-specific rates. None were a low probability event. Such considerations of variance suggest that the assumptions underlying the estimation of standard errors in the NCS may be too conservative. If this is the case, then less conservative assumptions would produce more year-to-year changes in the NCS that would be judged to be statistically significant. This, in turn, would reduce the number of situations where concern about sampling error leads parallel changes in the two trends to be treated as discrepant.

Procedural and Definitional Sources of Divergence

We will discuss here some major factors that could contribute to systematic discrepancies between the NCS and the UCR Crime Index. We will also document the magnitudes of these effects. Because of demographic trends during the seventies, as well as happenstance, the factors to be discussed tend mainly to make NCS rate changes diverge in the negative direction from the UCR during the period 1973 to 1979. In the eighties, some of the demographic trends that operated in this direction have turned about so that they elevated the NCS rates relative to the UCR Total Crime Index. The reversal was not sufficient, however, to offset factors possibly affecting the UCR that are not discussed here, so that NCS rates rose and the UCR rates declined. But it is likely that demographic trends will differentially affect the two series again and it is important to be in a position to be able to anticipate and to gauge these prospective future developments.

It is equally important to address the substantial changes that will occur in the design of both systems in the next decade and to specify the implications for the consistency of the NCS and UCR. Chapter 1 described the ambitious redesigns of both systems that will result in substantial changes in the procedures and definitions in the early nineties. We offer some conjectures regarding likely implications of these changes for the future consistency of the two indicators.

This chapter is, necessarily, a partial and preliminary attempt to understand discrepancies between the two series, as much of the information needed—especially information regarding their respective error structures —for a more complete investigation is not available. Consequently, our efforts are exclusively focused on those sources of discrepancy that are independent of the error structures of the two series. Moreover, we will not in every case be able to adjust the series for all potentially important definitional and procedural sources of divergence. For some of the factors, we will make simple direct adjustments of the series to see how they affect comparison of their changes over time. In other cases, we will go beyond simple adjustments for direct effects and attempt to adjust for the effects of the interaction of several factors. Where the data are not sufficient for such an adjustment, we will simply discuss the factor or factors in question and present rough estimates of direction and magnitude.

Comparison of the NCS and UCR is difficult given the complexity of the systems and the large number of differences between their respective definitions and procedures. Some differences of organization or method can have substantial effects on a given crime class, for example, rape which will not affect noticeably the comparability of the aggregate indicators when the class is a very small component of the total incidence.

Other differences in practice between the two data systems which can be great enough to influence the aggregate rates substantially may operate in mutually cancelling ways. For instance, the literal application of crime defining and counting algorithms by the NCS presumably results in counting as robberies many trivial but forcible takings of property (e.g. schoolboys robbed of their lunch money or marbles, intrafamilial property disputes, etc.) which police would be inclined to discount in the unlikely event that they did come to police attention. This relatively high NCS robbery count is offset by other features of the NCS, such as an overcorrection for multiple victim robberies, that reduce its count relative to the UCR.

The discussion that follows will emphasize those sources of discrepancy that have the potential to affect aggregate Index changes in ways that can be readily estimated using available data. Appendix A contains a more complete discussion of definitional and procedural differences that could influence the aggregate indicators as well as more specific differences that affect comparisons of particular index classes and subclasses.

Rate Bases

One of the most common failings in interpreting of trends in rates is to forget that much of the action is going on in the denominator of the rate, as well as in the numerator. Much of the discrepancy between NCS and UCR rates is due to the fact that they employ different bases for their rates. Just as rates that employ the same base will tend to track because of correlated change in their denominators, so changes in rates with different denominators can also diverge systematically.

NCS rates use two principal rate bases—eligible population and households—both different from the UCR Index's base, which is total resident population of the reporting areas.

For certain crimes, for example, burglary, household larceny and motor vehicle theft, the NCS uses the base of households, rather than population. A striking development in U.S. demography is the decline in the average size of households—down more than 12% during the life of the NCS—and a concomitant increase in the number of households. With households growing more rapidly than population, a time series of rates computed on a household base will diverge in a negative direction from one computed on a population base.

Between 1973 and 1986, the number of households in the United States rose from 69,337,000 to 90,138,000, an increase of 30% (BJS, 1988). During the same period, the denominator of the UCR rate, the total resident population, rose from 211,357,000 to 241,078,000, or only 14.1%. The magnitude of this discrepancy from 1973 to 1986 can be calculated as the ratio of the relative increases:

$$\frac{1.30}{1.141} = 1.139.$$

That is, the NCS household crime rates would be depressed by 13.9% over the period 1973 to 1986 relative to the UCR rates for comparable crime classes, due just to the different bases. The UCR classification scheme does not permit one to identify all components of the UCR Index that are treated as household crimes by the NCS. Therefore, to equate the two series with regard to rate bases, the NCS rates must be converted to a form comparable to the UCR. This requires converting NCS household crime-victimization rates to incident rates per 1,000 persons.

Using a common base for both the NCS household and personal crime rates allows the two types of crime to be aggregated into a combined Index in a form more directly comparable with the UCR. For personal crimes of rape and aggravated assault, NCS victimization rates have been used rather than incident rates because the former are comparable to UCR crime counting units (see Appendix A).[1]

Some of the movements of the NCS Personal Crime Rate in the seventies that ran contrary to changes in the UCR Total Crime Index—as were apparent in Figure 2.1—disappear when the combined NCS rate is plotted against the Index in Figure 2.2. Although the combined NCS has greater stability, the two series tend to rise and fall at the same points between 1973 to 1976, 1978 to 1979, and 1981 to 1984. They moved in contrary directions in 1977 to 1978, 1980, and 1984 to 1985.

The population base for NCS rates is the resident, noninstitutional population age 12 and over (or "the 12+ population"), the age range for which the NCS collects victimization information. UCR rates are computed on the base of the total resident population. The UCR records crimes against children under 12 years of age. These children as victims make some, but presumably scant, appearance in the crimes that form the numerator for the UCR. Whereas the U.S. population as a whole was increasing during the life of the NCS, the population under 12 years of age decreased continuously until 1985, when it began to increase.

Between 1973 and 1986, the 12+ population grew 20.9%, from 162,236,000 to 196,160,150 while the total resident population increased by only 14.1%. The larger increase in the NCS denominator will depress the NCS rate relative to the UCR. The ratio of the two relative increases is 1.059. That is, the NCS rate change between 1973 and 1986 for Index crimes was depressed relative to the UCR by 5.9% over that period simply as a result of the difference in the populations included in the denominator. Most of the effects (90%) of the faster growth of the 12+

---

[1] In this, and other analyses in this chapter, homicide is always excluded from the UCR Index. For obvious reasons, respondents in the NCS are not asked to report on homicide. Using proxy respondents was considered unwise.

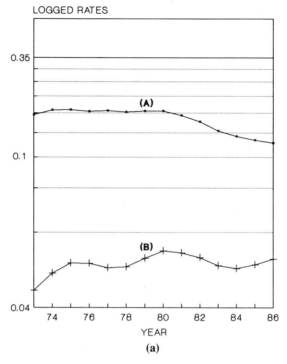

LOGGED RATES

(a)

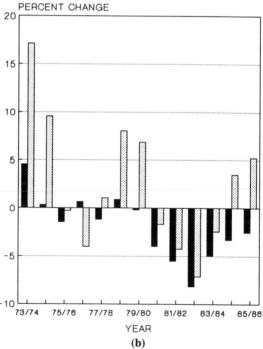

PERCENT CHANGE

(b)

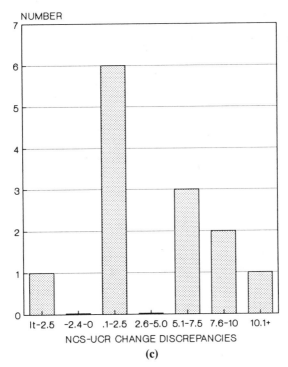

NUMBER

FIGURE 2.2. (a) Here, the NCS series is made more comparable with the official UCR (B) by combining NCS Personal and Household crimes (A) into an index using the population age 12 and over as the base. (b) In 5 out of 13 years, percent changes in the NCS (black bar) and UCR (dotted) move in opposite directions. (c) The differences between the annual changes in the series were positive and often large.

population relative to the total occurred in the period 1973 to 1979. The effects of restricting the UCR base for Index crimes to the age range of the NCS can be seen in Figure 2.3.

In addition to the effects of population dynamics on the base of the two rates, comparisons of the two series were affected by the population estimates that the FBI used for its rate bases during the intercensal period. Throughout intercensal periods, the Census Bureau estimates the total population using annual data on births, deaths, and immigration. When the intercensal estimates for the seventies were evaluated in the light of the 1980 Census, it turned out that they had become progressively more severe underestimates as the decade progressed. The FBI is only able to adjust the UCR retrospectively after a decennial Census to correct for the errors in the intercensal estimates it has used. There is a substantial effect on the UCR change measures in the year immediately following the decennial census as the UCR population figures successively

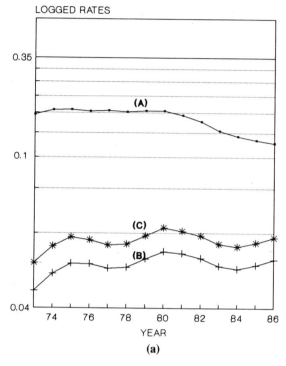

(a)

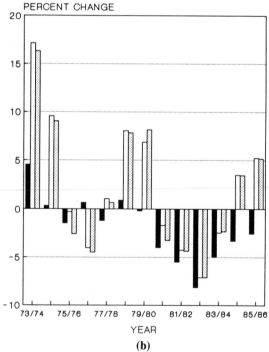

(b)

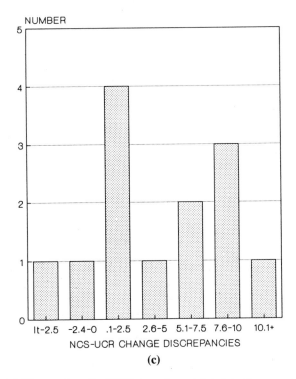

FIGURE 2.3. (a) Here, when the UCR base is restricted to the population age 12 and older, the UCR rates (C) are slightly less discrepant from NCS (A) combined rates, but the shape of the UCR series (B) is not greatly affected. (b) This adjustment to the UCR rates (dotted bar) makes the annual percentage change in the NCS (black bar) and UCR (white) more similar throughout the 1970s. (c) Overall, the frequency of larger differences in annual changes between the two series increased.

employ the first count and then the revisions issued by the Census. For the NCS, however, the effect is quite minor. That is because during the intercensal years, the numerator as well as the denominator of the rates are affected by the intercensal underestimate in that the sample ratio weights applied to each case entering the numerator and the denominator are based upon the population underestimates. Consequently, the underestimate of the population would affect the NCS rates only to the degree that there is differential underestimation of the population components for the weights. It seems clear that the UCR is much more systematically affected by errors in intercensal estimates.

The postcensally revised population figures showed a 6.3% increase from 1973 to 1979.[2] The original population estimates, used in the UCR

---

[2] Intercensal population misestimates at the time of writing had not been measured for the 1980s.

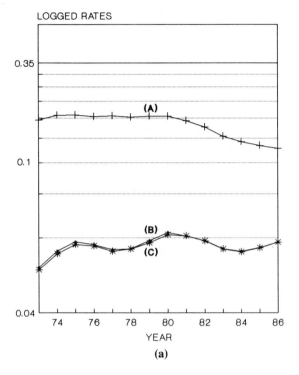

(a)

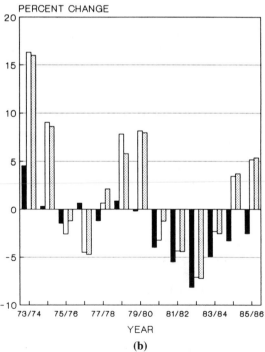

(b)

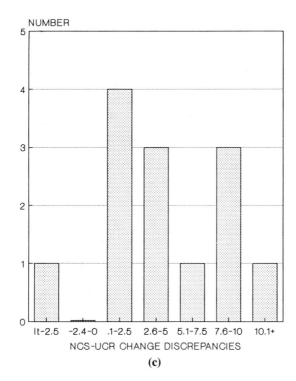

NUMBER

NCS-UCR CHANGE DISCREPANCIES

(c)

FIGURE 2.4. (a) The original UCR rates (B) involved an intercensal population underestimate that did not affect the NCS (A). The UCR rates differ somewhat less from the NCS when corrected retrospectively for the underestimate (C). (b) Using postcensally adjusted population as a base of the UCR rate (dotted bar) reduces the differences in the annual percentage change of the NCS (black) and the UCR (white). (c) This adjustment also reduces the frequency of large differences between change estimates in the two series.

publications, were 209,851,000 in 1973 and 220,099,000 in 1979, yielding an increase of only 4.9%. Thus, an additional discrepancy of rate changes of 1.3% (1.063/1.049 = 1.013) results from the use of the intercensal estimates in the UCR base (Figure 2.4).

The effects of all the factors we have discussed so far operate in the same direction. Specifically, each depresses the NCS rates relative to the UCR rates as the period from 1973 to 1979 progressed. In the 1980s, the growth in the 12+ population slowed as did the rate of household formation. This depressed the UCR relative to the NCS, although not enough to have the negative percent changes in the UCR exceed those of the NCS. The effects of intercensal misestimates of the population for the eighties cannot be assessed until after the 1990 Census, but they should be small for the early years of the decade included in our data.

TABLE 2.1. Sum of squared differences between annual percentage change in the NCS and UCR: Adjustments for rate-base differences.

Comparisons	Sum of squared differences	Cumulative percent change in SSD
NCS Index on a person base with UCR Index	494	—
NCS Index on a person base with UCR on 12+ base	478	−3.2
NCS Index on a person base with UCR on 12+ base intercensally adjusted	457	−7.4

The total effects of these differences in rate bases can be summarized as the sum of squared differences (SSD) between (1) the expected percent change in the UCR estimated from the percent changes in the NCS for the same period and (2) the percent change actually observed in the UCR rates. To the extent that adjustments in the UCR rate base reduce the SSD, they will have reduced the discrepancy of the two series. The SSD observed when predicting the annual percent change in the UCR Index crime rate from the change in the NCS rate is 494. Changing the UCR base to persons 12 years of age or older reduces the SSD by 3.2% to 478.[3] Correcting for the difference between the actual base and revised intercensal estimates of the number of persons 12 years and older reduces the SSD 4.2% to 457. The total effect of these rate base corrections is to reduce the SSD by 7.4%. Making the bases for the rates compatible and more accurate goes some way, therefore, toward explaining why the UCR rates during this period could be generally rising while the NCS rates remained relatively flat. In estimates of revised UCR rate changes in the subsequent sections of this chapter, we will incorporate, as relevant, these adjustments of the population denominators (see Table 2.1).

There are some differences between the base of the UCR and NCS rates that may be important, but the adjustments necessary to estimate their effect cannot be made at this time. The sampling frame of the NCS is, like the population base of the UCR, the resident population of the 50 states and the District of Columbia. (Although the UCR publishes data for Puerto Rico and U.S. territories, it does not include them in the Index totals.) The NCS excludes those persons who are crews of vessels, in institutions, or members of the armed forces living in barracks; the UCR

---

[3] In an earlier paper presented at the American Society of Criminology meetings in 1982, we reported the percent reduction in SSD as 6.1 for the adjustment of the UCR base to the population 12+. The change observed here is due to the fact that we have doubled the number of years in the trend and that the rate of increase in the 12+ population slowed in the 1980s.

includes them. Although most crimes occurring in these excluded habitations presumably would not be UCR-recorded (thefts in barracks, for example, handled by the military justice or disciplinary system, and most crimes by prison or mental institution inmates against each other or by the institutional authorities), victimizations of such excluded persons occurring outside the institutional setting would be included (as would offenses committed by such persons against in-frame victims in the NCS). The populations in question are concentrated in age ranges of extremely high victimization, so that, even though they comprise a very small percentage of the total population, the changes in their ratio to total population during the period under consideration could have some appreciable differential effect on the crime rates of the two series.[4] Because no means are available for estimating the relevant victimizations, we have not attempted to adjust for such discrepancies here.

The population base for UCR rates serves simply as a rough general measure of the size of the society for standardizing crime incidence, rather than, as in the case of the NCS, as a count of the exposed population for a true risk-rate measure. The population in the UCR denominator is not coterminous with the persons who can figure in crime incidents either as victims or as perpetrators.

For instance, it includes residents temporarily outside of the 50 states for short stays and it excludes foreign visitors. The latter component of the de facto population increased much more rapidly than the Census resident population during the period in question. The number of legal land entries per year of aliens from Canada and Mexico increased from an estimated 138 million to 170 million from 1973 to 1982 and the annual number of other nonimmigrants admitted more than doubled from 1970 to 1986—from 4.4 million to 10.6 million. Illegal entrants are also eligible to be victims or offenders of crimes known to the police. These sojourning foreigners are not balanced by increases in the foreign travel of U.S. residents. Americans travelling abroad increased only from about 6 million per year in 1973 to 7.8 million in 1979 and 8.5 million in 1982. Border crossings by U.S. citizens are estimated to have declined from about 100 million in 1973 to 93 million in 1979, but rose again in 1982 to 106 million. (See Bureau of the Census, 1986: 91–93, 238–240.) Lacking information on lengths of visits and consensus estimates with regard to illegal arrivals, one cannot make estimates of the discrepancy between the de facto at-risk population and the population estimates used by UCR and NCS. The discrepancy, however, appears to have increased appreciably particularly with regard to Mexico border movement. For personal crimes, various sources of evidence suggest that the traveller, sojourner and illegal immi-

---

[4] Rapid changes in the proportion of the young adult populations in these institutions, such as those that occur in military mobilizations and demobilizations, can have substantial effects on both series.

grant are at particularly high risk. An increasing supply of potential victims contributing to the numerator of UCR rates and not to its denominators appears to be an inestimable source of disproportionate increase of UCR rates over NCS rates, especially for the period 1973 to 1979.

Crimes Reported to the Police

The UCR is a measure of crimes known to the police; the NCS serves the purpose of providing data on crimes whether known to the police or not. Discrepancy of UCR from NCS can be regarded as inconsistency of the two series only insofar as comparison of the UCR is with that component of NCS rates involving crimes known to the police. In that the ratio of crimes known to the police to those not known varies among classes of crimes and of victims and these classes are found in variable ratio over time, the NCS and UCR total rates, if accurate, will diverge variably over time. These obvious facts have been recognized in a number of earlier efforts at comparing NCS and UCR series (Lehnen and Reiss, 1981).

If we simply compare the time series of NCS rates for incidents reported to the police with the UCR rates, adjusted to a comparable age-range and postcensally revised, extremely close correspondence is found for the two series (Figure 2.5). The difference between the series is reduced from an SSD of 457 for the comparison of the base-adjusted UCR with the NCS to an SSD of 191 for the comparison with the NCS restricted to incidents reported to the police (see Table 2.2). (The close correspondence in levels of these two series should not be construed as validation. The UCR incidence comes close to that of the NCS only because of the inclusion of crimes against businesses and organizations in the UCR rates that are not included in the NCS. The importance of this difference in scope of the two series will be examined further later in this chapter.)

We will seek to illuminate further how some of the dynamics of population change affect NCS and UCR series differently through effects on the proportion of crimes that are known to the police.

Because of the high relationship between the age of victim and reporting of incidents to the police, the changing age composition of the population which we have already considered as it affects the base of the rates is of special importance in the present context. During the years under consideration, the maturation of the "baby boom" generation made for particularly marked changes in the distribution of population in a small age span—an age span in which a marked increase takes place in the likelihood that an individual's victimization will be reported to the police. The greatest difference in reporting to the police is that between persons of high school age or younger and those above 20 years of age. According to the NCS, 32% of incidents involving teenage victims in 1973 were reported to the police as compared with 50% of the incidents involving

TABLE 2.2. Sum of squared differences between annual percentage change in the NCS and UCR: Adjustments for rate-base differences and NCS reported to the police.

Comparisons	Sum of squared differences	Cumulative percent change in SSD
NCS Index on a person base with UCR Index	494	—
NCS Index on a person base with UCR on 12+ base	457	−7.4
NCS reported to the police on a person base with UCR on 12+ base intercensally adjusted	191	−61.3

young adults (20 to 34) and 57% of those with older adult victims (35+). In the early years of the NCS, the average age within the under-35 age group was at a minimum. In the later seventies, the entire teenage component of the population fell sharply and the young adult population rose proportionately. As a consequence, progressively more of all victimizations would have been reported in the UCR and, ceterus paribus, the UCR rate would have increased more rapidly than the NCS rate. In the early 1980s, the proportion of the population in the low-reporting youthful age group fell.

The NCS also informs us that reporting to the police is related to the educational attainment of victims. Only 27% of the Index crimes involving persons with less than a high school education are reported to the police, whereas 36% of those involving high-school graduates and 35% of those involving college graduates are reported. Throughout the period 1973 to 1985, the educational attainment of the most highly victimized population component, that is, teenagers and young adults, increased such that more persons moved into high-reporting education groups by the end of the period. This increase was most pronounced between 1973 and 1980. It slowed considerably in the early eighties and the educational attainment of this age group began to decline in 1986. The increasing educational attainment of the teenage and young adult cohorts would be expected to exert upward influence on the proportion of all crimes known to the police.

Changes in the racial composition of the population may also affect reporting to the police, although not as much as changes in the age and educational-attainment distributions. In the NCS, nonwhites are slightly more likely to report victimizations to the police than whites, with 33.5% of incidents involving whites in 1975 reported to the police and 36.6% of incidents involving nonwhites. Racial differences in reporting are greater and more consistent for subclasses of crime such as robbery. Over the 1973 to 1985 period, the nonwhite population has increased faster than

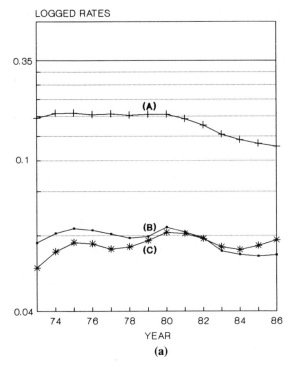

(a)

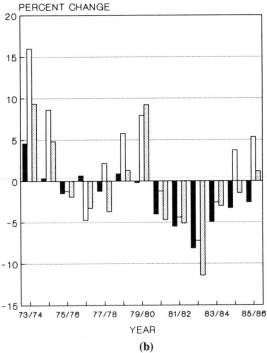

(b)

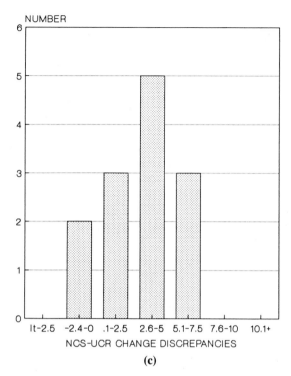

FIGURE 2.5. (a) The NCS combined rate series when restricted to incidents said to be reported to the police (C) corresponds more closely with the population adjusted UCR (B) than does the unrestricted NCS combined rate series (A). In recent years, the UCR actually exceeds the NCS rates for crimes known to the police. (b) The annual percentage changes in the NCS (black bar) increase in comparison to the UCR (white) when the numerator of the rate is restricted to crimes known to the police (dotted). In several years the direction of the change in the NCS is reversed. (c) As compared with Figure 2.4c, the distribution of UCR–NCS differences is displaced to the left when these adjustments are made.

the white population in the United States. In 1973, 11.7% of the U.S. population over 12 years of age was nonwhite, while in 1986 nonwhites comprised 14.1% of the population. This increase was even more pronounced in the heavily victimized teenage and young adult cohorts. In 1973, 13.9% of persons 12 to 15 were nonwhite, while in 1986 18.9% of this group were nonwhite.

It is unlikely that these demographic changes would operate additively in their effects on the number of crimes that become eligible for reporting in the UCR. Rather we would expect them to interact in complex ways. Indeed, we find this when we examine NCS victim subgroups defined by age, race and education. For example, older more highly educated, nonwhites, report crime to the police far less frequently than the additive effects of the individual demographic factors lead us to expect. For the purpose of estimating change in the pool of events eligible for reporting in the UCR and, thereby, expected change in the UCR, we will examine simple and direct effects as well as more complex interactive ones.

To illustrate the effects of shifts involving increases in the proportions of the population in demographic groups characterized by low reporting and proportionate increases in high reporting groups, let us assume that the victimization rates of every age and race group has remained the same since 1973. Further, let us assume that the UCR rate is a function of (1) the proportion of the population in high-and low-reporting age and race groups (p), (2) the group-specific victimization rate (v), which we have held constant at the 1973 rate, and (3) the group-specific rates of reporting to the police (r). Using NCS data, we estimate the expected UCR rate due to the growth in high-reporting groups for any year as

$$u = p_i * v_i * r_i,$$

where p_i is taken over the groups into which the population is divided, and the v_i and r_i are derived from the NCS. The expected percent change in the estimated UCR rate from one year to the next is

$$\frac{(u_{t+1} - u_t)}{u_t} \times 100.$$

This estimate of annual percent change will be used to predict the UCR annual rate from the observed UCR rate for 1973. The general model will be used to estimate expected change in the pool of incidents eligible for reporting in the UCR using age, race, and educational effects on reporting singly and in interaction. We will apply it in three specific models— two in which age, and race, respectively, are used to define the groups and one in which groups defined simultaneously by both their age and race characteristics will be used. Each model will provide an estimate of the percent change one could expect in the UCR if Index crime, as reported in the NCS, remained constant and changes occurred only in the demographic composition of the population and the proportions of incidents each group reported to the police.

A few caveats are in order in the use of NCS data in estimating these models. First, two of the parameters in this model—v_i and p_i—are affected by sampling errors that we have not estimated at this point. At high levels of aggregation, for example, national estimates of Index crimes, this sampling error is trivial. It may be somewhat larger for the group-specific parameters used in this model. Secondly, the models also assume that the population making up the UCR base has the same distributions for age and race characteristics as the NCS. However, the UCR population includes components excluded from NCS sampling frames. We know from previous comparisons of the UCR and NCS that the NCS estimate of the number of Index crimes said to be reported to

TABLE 2.3. Sum of squared differences in the annual percentage change in the UCR and the percentage change predicted by models using age, race, and reporting to the police 1973 to 1986.

Comparisons	Sum of squared differences	Cumulative percent change in SSD
UCR person crime rate with NCS person crime rate	747	0
UCR person crime rate with prediction using age, race, and reporting model	535	−29.7
UCR person crime rate with prediction using age and reporting model	533	−29.7
UCR person crime rate with prediction using race and reporting model	448	−40.0

the police is considerably higher than the number of Index crimes reported in the UCR for comparable periods. There are a number of reasons for this discrepancy, some of which will be discussed in this and subsequent chapters. The discrepency does not negate the usefulness of NCS data as a means of estimating the amount of change in the UCR, however, provided we are willing to assume for our immediate purposes that the NCS excess is in reasonably constant ratio to the UCR over time.

The crimes labeled household crimes by the NCS—burglary and motor vehicle theft—were not treated by the model because the design of the NCS and the nature of these crimes make it difficult to associate a particular household member (and therefore victim characteristics) with an incident. Larceny was included because the NCS ascribes most of its larcenies to a person rather than a household. Household larcenies had to be excluded, however, because the ability to discriminate these incidents within the larceny category is extremely poor given informational limitations of both the NCS and the UCR. (See Appendix A on the crime classes.) With some license, we label the crime types included in the comparison, "Individual Crimes." Figure 2.6 presents the 1973 to 1986 UCR rates for these crimes predicted by the age, race, and the interaction models, and, for comparison, the corresponding UCR rates adjusted to the base of the population 12 years and older.

The SSD between the annual percent change in the UCR individual crimes with base adjustments and the NCS individual crimes is 747. When the age and reporting model is used to predict percent annual change, the SSD is reduced to 535 or 29%. The simple race and reporting model reduces the SSD for personal crimes 40% to 448 (Table 2.3). The age, race, and reporting model reduces the SSD by 29% to 533. The interactive

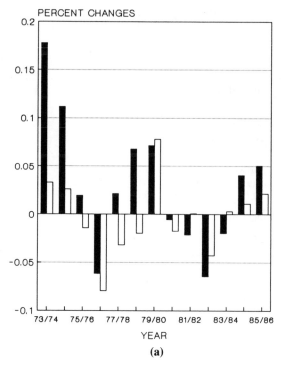

(a)

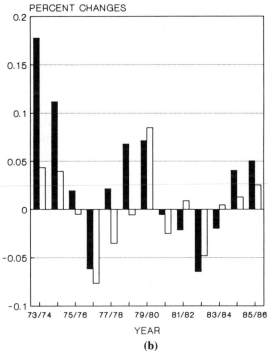

(b)

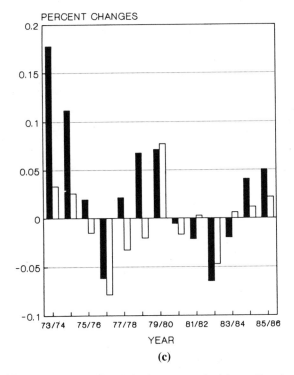

PERCENT CHANGES

YEAR

(c)

FIGURE 2.6. (a) UCR changes (black bar) compared with predicted changes from
an age-specific model based on 1973 victimization distributions and NCS-measured
yearly variation in rates of reporting victimization to the police (white). (b) UCR
changes (black bar) compared with predicted changes from a race-specific model
based on 1973 distributions of victimization and NCS-measured yearly variation in
rates of reporting victimization to the police (white). (c) UCR changes (black bar)
compared with changes predicted from an age and race-specific model based on
1973 distributions of victimization and NCS-measured variation in reporting victimization to the police (white).

model does not result in the same level of reduction, underscoring the
importance of race effects on reporting behavior in this period. Both the
base-adjusted UCR and the age-modeled predictions rise from 1973 to
1976, although the rise in the observed UCR is proportionately greater
than that of the predicted UCR. Both predicted and observed rates drop
in 1977, and remain relatively constant in 1978. The one major discrepancy between observed and predicted rates occurs in 1979 when the
observed UCR rate increases substantially and the estimated value remains essentially the same as in 1978.

The demographic changes in the foregoing analysis interact with changes
in the crime rate to affect reporting to the police. Models that do not
account for this interaction will misrepresent the reasons for divergent

change of the two indicators. In order to identify for each year the independent effects of change in each demographic variable on reporting to the police and, thereby, on the UCR requires a sample many times larger than that of the NCS. Moreover, our intention is not to develop a complete predictive model of changes in how many crimes will be reported to the police, but rather to suggest that some of the discrepancy of the series might have been anticipated simply by being attentive to the implications of demographic changes for crime reporting.

The Numerator of the Rates

The scope of crimes included in the numerator of the UCR rates is not identical to that of the NCS. In some cases, the differences in the numerators reflect deliberate restrictions of the scope of the NCS, whereas, in others, the nature of the data-collection method imposes certain limitations on one system that are not present in the other. The result is that these systematic differences in the definition of the numerator in each system can contribute to the discrepancy of the two trends over time.

Treatment of Commercial Crimes

The UCR includes in its numerator crimes involving commercial establishments, whereas the NCS excludes them from its incident counts. In the few instances that both a business and a personal victimization occur in the same incident, NCS excludes the case from its incident count although counting it for victimization rates.

NCS also includes victimizations of "unrecognizable businesses" conducted from residences. The UCR Handbook has no rule covering these ambiguous cases and some of them may be classified as nonresidential. We lack information on the importance of crimes against businesses conducted from residences in the two series and the variability of their treatment as business or residential crimes.

Throughout the period 1973 to 1986, crimes that the NCS would not include constitute a substantial, but inestimable, proportion of all robberies, burglaries, and larcenies in the UCR. Appendix A discusses the extent to which it is possible to identify some subclasses of UCR crimes as wholly or largely composed of crimes against the property of businesses or other organizations. On the average, 27% of the robberies reported in the UCR, 37% of the burglaries and 12% of the larcenies were in such subclasses. Thefts of commercial and personal motor vehicles are not differentiated in the UCR, but, as indicated in Appendix A, other data can be used to provide a rough estimate of commercial vehicles included in the UCR. On average, 17.5% of crimes reported in the UCR are identifiable as commercial crimes. When the UCR subclasses that definitionally encompass commercial victimizations are eliminated and the re-

TABLE 2.4. Sum of squared differences between actual percentage change in the NCS and UCR: Adjustments for rate-base differences, UCR excluding commercial crimes, and NCS reported to the police and excluding series incidents and identifiable commercial crimes.

Comparisons	Sum of squared differences	Cumulative percent change in SSD
NCS Reported to the police with UCR on 12+ base and intercensally adjusted	191	—
UCR on 12+ base and intercensally adjusted excluding commercial crimes with the NCS reported to the police	178	−6.8

sulting rates compared with NCS rates for crimes known to the police, the two series do track more closely (Figure 2.7).

The SSD between annual percent change in the two series is reduced somewhat more when commercial incidents are excluded than when they are included in the UCR. The SSD for the comparison of NCS crimes reported to the police and the base-adjusted UCR which is 191, decreases to 178 when identifiable commercial crimes are excluded from the UCR series (see Table 2.4).

Figure 2.7 also corrects the impression left by Figure 2.6 that the UCR, base adjusted, and the NCS police-reported series show essentially the same rate for 1979, 1981, and 1982 and that the UCR rates are higher from 1983 to 1986. Once the identifiable portions of the commercial crimes are removed from the UCR, we can see that a considerable difference remains in the level of crime indicated by the two series. Nonetheless, when these various adjustments are made, the two series seem to be converging over time. The differences between level estimates in the adjusted NCS and the adjusted UCR are greater in 1973 than in 1986. Over time the rate of Index crimes reported to the police has declined in the NCS while the Index rate in the UCR has increased.

The secular movement of total Index crimes in the NCS has been downward, but the proportion of crimes reported to the police in the NCS has steadily increased. Consequently, an increasing proportion of crimes included in the survey are also presumably included in the UCR by virtue of their being known to the police.

Unfounded Crime in the UCR

The NCS and UCR employ quite different modes of data collection, each of which has its own strengths and weaknesses and requires specific procedural definitions for handling aberrant or problem cases. The UCR,

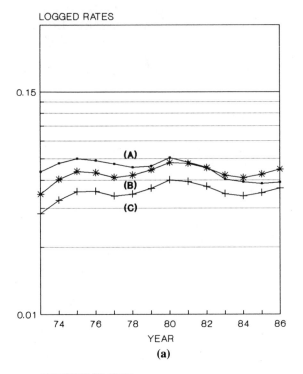

LOGGED RATES

(a)

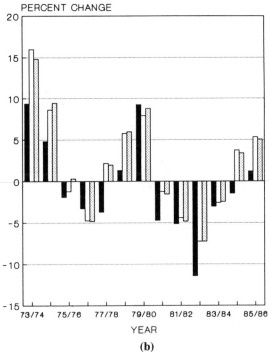

PERCENT CHANGE

(b)

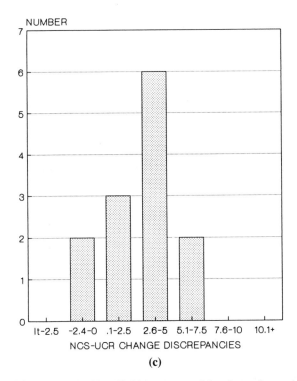

NUMBER

NCS-UCR CHANGE DISCREPANCIES

(c)

FIGURE 2.7. (a) Excluding identifiable commercial crimes from the UCR (C) counters the pattern of Figure 2.5a in which the UCR Rates (B) exceed those of the NCS for crimes known to the police (A). The shape of the adjusted UCR, however, varies little from the unadjusted. (b) With this adjustment in the UCR (dotted bar), the annual percent changes in the UCR (white) are made more similar to the NCS (black) in the 1980s. (c) The magnitudes of the differences between annual percent change in the two series tend to be smaller when identifiable commercial crimes are excluded from the UCR.

for instance, is an administrative series that is a byproduct of record-keeping systems designed to serve local police departments in the performance of their routine duties. One of the principal purposes of these systems is the presentation of evidence leading to prosecution and the record systems are closely tied to the investigative process. The UCR is able to take advantage of the definitions and procedures of the investigative process. Specifically, if a crime is reported to the police, but later investigation establishes that no crime occurred or was attempted, the incident is unfounded and is excluded from the UCR published reports. The NCS, on the other hand, relies upon the victim's account to determine whether a crime has occurred and therefore may include a number of events that would be unfounded in the UCR. Doubtless, there are instances in which police find no basis for, or "unfound" reports while victims may continue to believe crimes occurred, which they would report to an NCS interviewer. The victim may be persuaded by the same subsequent evidence that led police to dismiss the report and indeed may be the source of that evidence, for instance, where a victim contradicts a report originally made by a third party or where an object reported as stolen is later found to have been mislaid or innocently borrowed.

Although the UCR collects data on crimes that were unfounded, they do not process or tabulate these data on an annual basis. Consequently, it is difficult to estimate what the effects would be on series change were different evidentiary standards to be used for including events in the numerator of the rates. A special study conducted by the UCR (Federal Bureau of Investigation, 1974) suggests that approximately 4% of crimes reported as Index crimes in the UCR are unfounded at a later time. There is also little reason to expect that there is much systematic variation over time in the effects of unfounding on divergences of the two series. A second study of unfounding done in 1977 showed essentially the same levels of unfounding.[5]

Series Victimization in the NCS

Because the NCS relies almost exclusively on the accounts of respondents to define crimes and criminal victimization, procedures and rules were developed for dealing with situations in which demands for information in the survey overtax the respondent. Special provisions were needed to deal with instances in which ordinary survey procedures fail to yield an interview record with all of the information essential for determining:

1. whether a crime has occurred,
2. if so, the type of crime, and
3. the exact count of crimes applicable to the experience related by the respondent.

One such procedure that may influence the relative movements of the two indicators over time is the NCS treatment of certain kinds of experience recorded on a single Incident Report Form as "series victimizations."

How to treat interviewee's accounts that do not accord neatly with the concept of the discrete incident at a point in time has been problematic since the first explorations of victimization survey methodology. Biderman, et al. (1967) originally viewed the problem as follows:

Series of Like Offenses.—A difficulty involving [counting] units that could not be solved satisfactorily was encountered in the present study. This occurred where a

---

[5] Personal communication with Paul Zolbe who was, at the time, the chief of the Uniform Crime Reporting Program.

respondent described what actually was a series of related acts over a period of time, where each could be classed as an offense, but where the individual either could not specify precisely how many times the offense had taken place or where so many separate instances were involved that such acts, if counted individually, would contribute highly disproportionately to the total picture of victimization at which the study aimed. . . . Usually, the victim assumed or knew the series of offenses was being committed by the same offender or group of offenders. In each instance where the respondent spoke of the matter in terms of a unitary series of identical offenses of one of the types listed above, it has been considered a single incident. This has been done even though the victim may have made two or more complaints to the police on different occasions. In this respect, consequently, the survey may lead to an undercount relative to police statistics. (pp. 70–71)

The NCS defines "series victimizations" somewhat differently:

Three or more criminal acts that are similar if not identical in nature and incurred by individuals who are unable to identify separately the details of each act or recount accurately the total number of such acts. . . . (Bureau of Justice Statistics, 1986:113)[6]

To deal with accounts fitting into the "series of victimizations" definitions, the interviewer is instructed (1) to record the number of events reported, (2) to date these events by quarter, and (3) to collect detailed information on the most recent incident only. Series incidents are not used in computing NCS incidence rates (Dodge, 1987). A major reason for their exclusion is that the NCS annual rate calculations require dating of incidents to a specific month of the year.

If the proportion of NCS crime incidents that were treated using the "series incident" procedure has changed over the life of the survey, the decision to exclude such victimizations from rate computation may affect the comparability of change measures for the UCR and the NCS.

The choice of an approach to adjusting the NCS so as to include incidents reported as a series depends upon our assumptions about the appropriateness of using data on the most recent incident in the series to characterize all incidents in the series. If we assume that the incidents

---

[6] This NCS definition does not encompass the full range of victimization recounting that cannot be dealt with adequately as discrete, brief incidents. Biderman (1981:795), for instance, discusses crimes whose commission has extensive duration in time such as the worker who is kept in line by union or company goons, the merchant terrorized by a shakedown racket, the prostitute by a pimp, the spouse or sexual partner kept from separating from a hated relationship by fear of violence and various other not uncommon examples. The NCS series procedure also does not provide for the person whose work role or some other status involves extremely frequent exposure to assault. Many policemen, for instance, are so frequently targets of violence as to make it burdensome for them to try to recall, "How many times in the past six months. . . ?"

reported in each series would, with rare exception, fall within the same type of crime classification, then we could safely count as separate crimes each of the incidents lumped together by the NCS as a single "series incident"; thereby substantially increasing the numerators in calculating rates. If, however, we assume that since the NCS prescribes that descriptive details be collected only of the most recent event of a series, then only this incident of the series can be safely included in the numerator. We will adjust the NCS rates under both assumptions to determine possible effects of the treatment of series incidents as single incidents on the discrepancies in change estimates (Figure 2.8).

Under the most conservative of the assumptions above, only one incident would be added to the NCS rate numerator for each series incident.

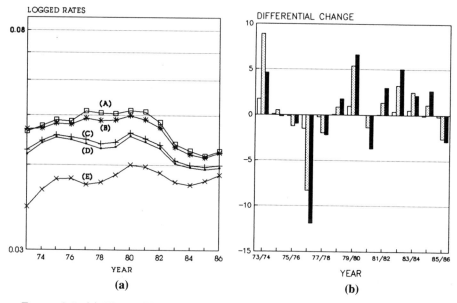

FIGURE 2.8. (a) Three different ways were used to add "series incidents" to the numerator of NCS rates: Each series is included as one incident (C); the mid-value is taken as the class value for class intervals of the number of incidents of a series (B); post-1978 distributions of the actual number of events in a series are extrapolated to estimate class values for earlier years (A). These adjusted rates are compared to the NCS rates that exclude "series incidents" (D) and to the UCR (E). (b) Differences in annual changes in the UCR and the NCS without series are compared to differences in the annual changes in the two rates using the three different series counting methods; differences in change between the unadjusted rates minus the differences including series as one incident (white bar); as the midpoint (dotted); as an extrapolation of post-1978 data (black). Discrepancies are smaller in recent years.

TABLE 2.5. Sum of squared differences between actual percentage change in the NCS and UCR: Adjustments for rate-base differences, UCR excluding commercial crimes, and NCS reported to the police and including series incidents in three different ways.

Comparisons	Sum of squared differences	Cumulative percent change in SSD
UCR on 12+ base and intercensally adjusted excluding commercial crimes with the NCS reported to the police	178	—
UCR on 12+ base and intercensally adjusted excluding commercial crimes, and NCS reported to police with each series incident weighted as 1	207	+14
UCR on 12+ base and intercensally adjusted excluding commercial crimes, and NCS reported to police with each series incident weighted as midpoint of the interval	505	+184
UCR on 12+ base and intercensally adjusted excluding commercial crimes, and NCS reported to police with each series incident weighted as single year intervals	557	+212

The NCS police-reported Index crime rate would, thereby, be increased an average of 3.8%. The 1973 rate would be most affected by this procedure—4.8%—and 1979 rate would be increased the least—3.4%. Including series incidents in the NCS in this fashion, however, does not improve the overall fit between the NCS and UCR time series. The SSD between annual percent change in the UCR and annual percent change in the NCS with each series counted as a single incident is larger than the SSD between UCR and the NCS with series excluded (see Table 2.5).

Adjusting the NCS trends for series incidents under the less conservative assumption—that all incidents included in the series should be counted—was done in two ways because of changes made in the NCS instrument in 1979. Specifically, prior to 1979 the NCS incident questionaire grouped data on the number of events or crimes in a series into three class intervals: 3 to 4, 5 to 10, and more than 10. After 1979, interviewers recorded the exact number of crimes that respondents said were in the series. One set of adjustments of the pre-1979 data was made using the interval data. The number of crimes in a series was assumed to be the midpoint of the interval in which the incident was reported. An incident in the 3-to-4 interval, for example, was assumed to include 3.5 crimes, a series in the 5-to-10 interval was scored as 7.5 crimes, and so forth. The number of series incidents in a given year was obtained by multiplying each series by the midpoint value of that interval and summing across intervals. The post-1979 data were grouped into intervals similar to those for the pre-1979 data.

A second set of adjustments was made, taking advantage of the additional information available after 1979. For the post-1979 period the total number of series crimes was obtained by multiplying each report by the number of incidents in the series. For the pre-1979 period, the data from the post-1979 period were used to estimate the distribution of series crimes within the class intervals. These estimated distributions, in turn, were used to estimate the intraclass frequency distributions of series crimes for each year prior to 1979.

When these three methods for estimating the number of incidents in series crimes are used to adjust the NCS numerator, the NCS and UCR time series become more dissimilar than they did with series excluded. Moreover, the fit between the two series is worse when the estimated number of crimes in a series is used rather than treating each series crime as a single event. The SSD increases from 178 to 207, or 14%, when series crimes are included as single events. When the number of incidents in a series is factored into the adjustment as the midpoint of the frequency interval, the SSD increases, by 184%, to 505. When the second series adjustment is applied to the NCS rates, the SSD increases again to 557, or 212% higher than it was when series crimes were excluded (see Table 2.5).

It is also clear from Figure 2.8 that the NCS series is less stable when series crimes are included. This instability is modest when only one crime is counted for each series of victimizations. The time series retains the same general shape that it had when series were excluded. The SSD is greater than it is when series victimizations are excluded because when the series crimes are included the drop in NCS rates between 1976 and 1977 become smaller and the gain for 1978–1979 larger. The irregularities in the NCS series increase substantially when estimates of the number of incidents in a series are added to the rates. Much of the worsening in fit comes from there having been smaller increases for 1973 to 1974 than were observed in the time series excluding series crimes as well as from large increases between 1976 and 1977, an interval in which there was a falloff in the rate unadjusted for series.

Comparisons of Most Comparable Subclasses

Deleting only the most unambiguously commercial subclasses from the UCR, as we did earlier in this chapter, retains many incidents in the numerator of the UCR that are out of the scope of the NCS. By comparing rates constructed of just those crime classes and subclasses that can be assumed to have reasonable congruence of definition and scope for the two systems, we can put to some test the implicit expectation that levels of the crimes excluded from the NCS will fluctuate from year to year in relatively constant ratio to those included. Appendix A discusses in detail these issues of comparability. The most comparable classes are Aggravated Assault and Rape, along with the Pocketpicking and Purse-snatching subclasses of larceny. We can also accept UCR Residence Burglary as reasonably comparable to NCS burglaries, although the UCR contains in unknown proportions burglaries of hotels, motels, and so forth. For precision, a small number of NCS incidents have to be included in which simple assaults occurred together with a breaking-and-entering, in order to reflect the priority that the NCS assigns to the assault over the burglary category in such incidents. With rather greater imprecision, we will also add UCR Motor-Vehicle Theft to the comparable classes since, as discussed in Appendix A, we are able to conclude that the bulk of these thefts involve household property and we are able to arrive at a rough estimate of the proportion of the class that does. Specifying the comparable classes in this way excludes from the comparison the bulk of the Larceny class and the entire Robbery class. As discussed in Appendix A, we find the UCR Robbery class suspect with regard to the comparability of its scope to that of NCS robbery category.

The components of the UCR we regard as most comparable to crimes within the scope of the NCS make up a varying proportion of the total UCR Index from year to year (Table 2.6). The corresponding types of crime in the NCS also vary considerably over time as a proportion of all NCS police-reported incidents. In large measure, these fluctuations are due less to the temporal variablity of the categories of crimes that are retained for the comparisons than to the variabilitity of categories we have excluded. Eliminating most of the Larceny-Theft class, in particular removes a class that displays pronounced temporal change and which is so numerous as to have major influence on the aggregate rate. The ratio of the most comparable components of each series to the total crimes for that series varies over time, generally in inverse relationship to the total level. This reflects the degree to which variations in larceny determine change in the total crime rate for both the NCS and the UCR.

By the SSD criterion, there is less correspondence of rate changes in the NCS and UCR series after restricting comparisons to the most comparable commercial crimes than when only the clearly commercial categories were deleted. The SSD increases from 178 to 325 (see Table 2.7). Again, the year 1973 contributes disproportionately to the SSD, but even when the 1973-1974 change is omitted from comparison, the SSD for the most comparable components exceeds that of the earlier analysis. The

TABLE 2.6. Ratios of most comparable crimes to index crimes for NCS police-reported with crime series included and for UCR: 1973 to 1986.

Ratio	Year						
	1973	1974	1975	1976	1977	1978	1979
NCS most comparable/ NCS police-reported	.476	.452	.438	.427	.440	.439	.439
UCR most comparable	.340	.328	.320	.306	.316	.323	.316

Ratio	Year						
	1980	1981	1982	1983	1984	1985	1986
NCS most comparable/ NCS police-reported	.443	.456	.440	.434	.435	.440	.445
UCR most comparable	.326	.321	.311	.311	.314	.314	.321

general shape of the two series remains much as previously observed (see Figure 2.9).

If the divergences of the UCR time series from the NCS's are driven largely by components of the UCR that are out of scope for the NCS, these must be those incidents in the NCS we are unable to isolate. It is possible that the assumption that the UCR and NCS rates stay in constant ratio over time may not hold within the large and ambiguous larceny class and the robbery classes even though it may hold fairly well for changes in classes more clearly identifiable as to whether they are in scope for the NCS.

Implications of the UCR and NCS Redesigns for Divergence

This chapter thus far has dealt with data from the two surveys for years 1973 through 1986. Both the NCS and the UCR have recently undergone extensive evaluation and redesign. Although the final outlines of the changes have not been set, it may be useful to speculate about how expected alterations in the two systems may affect their future consistency.

Implications of the UCR Redesign

Although the full implementation of the new UCR system will take considerable time, the changes proposed will extend considerably our ability to identify the degree to which the UCR is or is not counting equivalently the same phenomenon as the NCS. The most important

TABLE 2.7. Sum of squared differences between actual percentage change in the NCS and UCR: Adjustments for rate-base differences, UCR excluding commercial crimes, and NCS reported to the police, UCR most comparable, NCS most comparable.

Comparisons	Sum of squared differences	Cumulative percent change in SSD
UCR on 12+ base and intercensally adjusted excluding commercial crimes with the NCS reported to the police	178	—
UCR most comparable crimes on a 12+, intercensally adjusted base, NCS comparable crimes reported to the police excluding series	325	+82

feature of the UCR Redesign is a change from a summary system with highly preaggregated recording to an incident-based data system. This data will put the UCR into a form much more like that of the NCS than is the summary system still in use. In addition, information elements are to be added that will extend the range of possible comparisons of UCR and NCS data. The change from a summary to an incident-based system will permit much more flexible use of the UCR data than is currently possible. The additional information available in the redesigned system will make it possible to identify more precisely those offenses counted in the UCR that would also be eligible for counting in the NCS.

An incident-based UCR will permit adjustments to the type that previously could only be made to the NCS. Rather than being restricted to rates for the broad published classes, we will be able to consider the relation of any of a large number of the attributes of a UCR event, alone or in combinations, to whether and how that event would figure in NCS incidence estimation. Our ability to use this new flexibility in UCR data will depend on how the data are made available. Incident-level data on public-use tapes or disks would be preferable for researchers exploring NCS–UCR comparability.

The new information available in the redesigned UCR will substantially improve our ability to identify the most definitionally and procedurally comparable subclasses of events in the two series. Two major improvements that are to be implemented specifically for the purpose of enhancing NCS–UCR comparability are the identification of (1) incidents involving businesses or other corporate entities, exclusively; and (2) crimes befalling persons under 12 years of age.

Our analyses in this book were particularly hampered by our inability to identify commercial crimes in the UCR exhaustively. The new program provides a code for type of victim in the incident report so as to distinguish private individuals as victims from businesses, governments, finan-

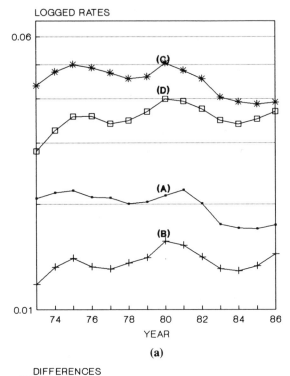

(a)

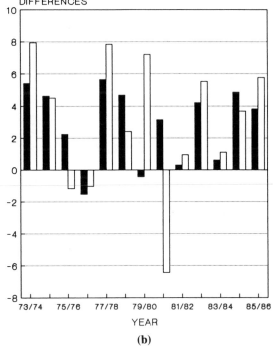

(b)

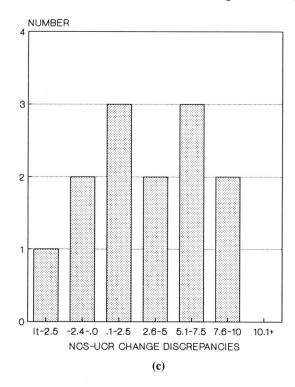

FIGURE 2.9. (a) When the NCS rate (C) for crimes known to the police and the UCR index (D) are each restricted to the most definitionally comparable categories (A and B, respectively), the congruence of the two trends is reduced. (b) Annual changes in rates for the "most comparable" categories (white bar) differ substantially, but erratically from those for total index crimes (black). (c) Restricting the two series to the "most comparable" categories makes the rate changes of the two series more discrepant.

cial institutions, religious organizations, and society in the abstract (the last to be used for traditional victimless crimes) (Federal Bureau of Investigation, 1988b). The ability to identify commercial crimes in the UCR should be substantially improved thereby.

Another serious impediment has been our inability to identify UCR crimes in which the victim was under 12 years of age and that, with certain exceptions, would therefore not be eligible for the NCS. The new UCR provides data on the age of the victim in single years.

The ability to explore UCR–NCS comparison should also be enhanced by modification of the hierarchy rule. The redesigned UCR will not require the mutually exclusive, hierarchical application of offense categories to events involving multiple UCR offenses. That each class of offense in any incident will be coded will enhance our ability to equate published UCR and NCS rates where these involve crime classifications following the slightly different hierarchical rules used by each system. Recall, for instance, that we treated some simple assaults in the NCS data as burglaries for our analysis because the UCR hierarchy rule gives precedence in classification to burglary over simple assault.

The UCR's "hotel rule" treats a property crime that occurs to more than one dwelling unit in a multiple-unit structure as a single incident. This is done to avoid double reporting by both individual occupants and by the management of the structure, the assumption being that the management would be the usual notifier of the police in such events. The victimization of each unit is eligible for counting by the NCS as a separate incident. The redesigned UCR retains the hotel rule, but participating jurisdictions are to indicate the number of premises entered when the rule is being applied to a burglary (Federal Bureau of Investigation, 1988b). This information will permit more logical equating of UCR to NCS burglary incidence.

Our ability to explore the consistency of the two systems would have been improved if the redesigned UCR were to treat somewhat differently the new information on residential status of the victim. The data-collection guidelines for the new system distinguish between persons who are residents and those who are nonresidents of the jurisdiction in which the crime occurred. This information is necessary for computing risk rates for residents of particular jurisdictions uncontaminated by victimizations of commuters, tourists and other nonresidents. For national crime rates, as contrasted with subnational uses, the only residential distinction essential for enhancing NCS-UCR comparability is that between residents and non-residents of the United States.[7] As we suggested earlier in this chapter, the UCR includes offenses against foreign visitors in unknown proportion. Alteration of UCR data-collection guidelines to identify U.S. residence would increase the possibilities for constructing valid NCS–UCR comparisons.

Overall, the redesigned UCR should greatly improve our ability to explore and understand the sources of inconsistencies between the NCS and the UCR, when and if the redesign is implemented in a fashion consistent with the *Blueprint for the Future of the Uniform Crime Reporting Program* (BJS, 1985). We need not await full implementation of the new system to reap the benefits of the changes outlined above. Even data for one or several large states would provide some estimates of the

---

[7] Foreign nationals working or living in the United States are interviewed in the NCS, but other foreign nationals are excluded, since they are not part of the resident population by definition.

importance of some sources of discrepancies that we could only guess at in the foregoing analysis.

Implications of the NCS Redesign

The effect of the NCS Redesign on the comparability of the National aggregate rates is much less clear. In one respect, there is less room for improvements than in the case of the UCR redesign because the survey is already a detailed and highly disaggregated data system that can be manipulated extensively to enhance comparability with external data sources. Some of the near and long term changes in the NCS for improving the survey's scope and accuracy are likely to increase the proportion of crimes reported in the NCS that are not routinely captured in the UCR. For example, changing from proxy to direct interviewing of 12 and 13 year olds may substantially increase the reporting of crimes occurring in school—crimes that are not usually reported to the police. Similarly, including vandalism in the NCS may encourage the reporting of more attempted burglaries which are often not reported to the police. Presumably, restricting NCS–UCR comparisons to crimes reported to the police should lessen the effect of incorporating these changes. The Redesign will have the opposite effect, however, if it results in a relatively large increment in the types of incidents that are routinely unfounded or downgraded by the police.

The near term redesign of the NCS will contribute materially to interseries comparisons by providing more extensive information on the response of the criminal justice system to the incident. Prior to the implementation of the near term changes, it was possible to identify incidents that citizens reported to the police, but one could not determine which of these incidents were recorded as crimes by the police. The redesigned NCS asks whether there was contact with the police and if a police report was completed for the incident.[8] If we assume that respondents can reliably determine those incidents that became a matter of police record and, therefore which could figure in the UCR, this information could be used in place of the current NCS reporting item to yield an NCS data subset for comparison with the UCR. The data from respondents on police recording also might shed some light on police practices with regard to the unfounding of complaints.

Subnational comparisons of the NCS and UCR may be improved by changes in the geographic identifiers used in the survey.

---

[8] For a listing of the questions on police service included in the implementation of the near term changes in the NCS see Whitaker (1989).

Summary

Periodically, the UCR Index Crime time series has moved in directions opposite to movements of the NCS. These discrepancies gave rise to debates about which of the two systems offers a better measure of crime. We have suggested that the discrepancy in considerable measure has been more apparent than real. The impression that the series were in conflict stemmed from a failure to take into account major definitional and procedural differences between the NCS and the UCR. These are differences that could cause the two indicators to move in different directions when neither is in error. We presented some of the major procedural differences between the two systems and estimated the magnitude of their effect on interseries comparisons for the period from 1973 to 1986.

Some of the discrepancy in the two trends follows from differences between the bases on which the systems calculate their rates. The UCR rates are based on the total population of the United States, whereas the NCS uses households and persons over 12 years of age as rate bases. When these populations change at different rates over time, the two trends will diverge even were the numerators of the rates to remain the same. We were able to adjust for some of these rate-base differences. For the period 1973 to 1986 the adjustments by which we attempted to make the rate bases more similar improved the correspondence of the two trends. These adjustments involved substituting the poulation of persons as a base where the NCS used households, truncating the UCR population at age 12 to conform to the NCS, and using post-censally adjusted population estimates.

We had no means for dealing with one type of inconsistency between the rates of the two systems. The NCS population base is theoretically the same as the at-risk population whose victimizations figure into the rate numerator. In the case of the UCR, however, the population base does not include foreign vistiors who are contributing to the numerator, either as victim or perpetrator, some inestimable number of incidents.

Differences between the scope of the numerators of the NCS and the UCR also may be responsible for the inconsistent movements of the two time series. Excluding crimes reported to the police from the NCS improves the correspondence of the trends substantially. A similar although less dramatic effect follows from deleting identifiable commercial crimes from the UCR. Conversely, counting separately incidents making up NCS "series incidents" fails to bring the two series into closer accord. When the comparison between the two time series are restricted to those classes of crimes reported in each that we identified as most comparable in definition and procedure, the discrepancy between the two series becomes more pronounced. We are severely limited, however, in our ability to isolate within the data of the two systems, and particularly in the highly aggregated data of the UCR, those types of incidents that are defined and treated fairly comparably by both agencies. The conversion of the UCR into an incident-based system and the systematic identification of commercial crimes within that system will make possible much more refined adjustments of the series for differences between them in scope, definition and procedure.

3
The Importance of Nonuniformities in Measurement for the Appearance of Divergence

Once we have applied the adjustments that appear useful for dealing with procedural anomalies and definitional incongruities between the NCS and UCR, the two series correspond much more closely. Nonetheless, major discrepancies between the series remain even when we restrict their scope to those crimes that are most comparable definitionally and procedurally. As social indicators, the two systems would sometimes have sent conflicting signals about crime during the period studied even had their reporting embodied the kinds of adjustments we have been able to make for these definitional and procedural differences. Undoubtedly, more precise and complete information on incidents that are out of scope in one series, but present in the other would further our understanding of these divergences. Some of their lack of accord may be due to the nonuniform application of definitions and procedures, to changes in procedures or to expedients that were adopted to facilitate data collection but which introduced series correlated measurement effects. For instance, UCR participating agencies that progressively report more multiple burglaries in a motel as separate incidents have misapplied the "hotel" rule and introduced nonuniformity of the first type. The substantial increase in telephone interviewing in the NCS since 1979 is an illustration of a procedural change that could affect series comparability. The decision to include data from "unbounded" interviews with residents of sampled units in making NCS estimates is illustrative of the third type of nonuniformity. This expedient was adopted even though it was known that the resulting estimates would be systematically higher than would be the case were the "bounding" restriction uniformly applied. As a consequence, NCS series variation has been artifactually influenced by changing rates of old to new households as this ratio, in turn, was affected by changing rates of social mobility and new household formation during the period in question (Biderman and Cantor, 1984).

We also have good reason to believe that influences of the foregoing kinds on the two indicators are at most partially mutually offsetting, and also that they have not remained in constant ratio over time and, there-fore, that they have contributed systematically to series divergence.

Although this chapter deals with matters conventionally termed "mea-surement error" or "nonsampling error," we prefer to avoid use of the word "error" here. To speak in terms of "error" would imply that there is an unambiguous "true value" and some generally agreed upon measure of it against which the NCS and UCR could be evaluated. Unfortunately, this is not the case. In the present work, we can usually assess "errors" only as departures from stated definitions or procedures used in the two series. In some instances, we can evaluate data from either or both of the systems in terms of their plausibilty or consistency.

This chapter builds upon our earlier work on definitional and proce-dural sources of discrepancy and begins to explore the effects of measure-ment variability upon the series. It examines major types of measurement anomalies that are found in the NCS and UCR. Using some information now available on measurement problems in the NCS, we specify the direction and magnitude of their effects on the aggregate rate estimates the NCS publishes. Simple adjustments are made in the series for major sources of measurement variability and these adjusted trends are com-pared to assess the impact of measurement effects on the two series.

Nonuniformity in the NCS and UCR

In a sample-based system such as the NCS, it is conventional among survey statisticians to speak of two major subcategories of error—"sampling error" and "nonsampling error." In census systems such as the UCR, all error by definition is "nonsampling error." The UCR system, however, falls short of being a 100% sample. Although the proportion of police departments participating in the UCR system has grown over the years to a reported 85% encompassing 96% of the population, not all jurisdictions make returns for every reporting period. In addition, the reports of some jurisdictions are regarded as suspect and are dropped from the tabula-tions for the period in question. The FBI uses imputation to deal with substantial problems of missing offense data each year. The UCR, in other words, is affected by the equivalent of the unit noncompletions that in sample survey system, such as the NCS, are treated as a component of the statistical error of their estimates.

NCS estimates for specific classes of crime and particular population components are subject to substantial sampling error. The most popular and influential uses of the NCS and the UCR, however, are captured by headline phrases suggesting: "U.S. Crime is Up," or "U.S. Crime is Down." For the NCS rates pertinent to such questions, which are based on aggregates of data for all classes of persons and crimes, sampling error is of relatively modest importance. This chapter focuses on such highly aggregated rate estimates.

Procedural variability, however, affects both the NCS and the UCR and there are no well-developed bodies of theoretical knowledge that can be used to eliminate entirely these nonuniformities or to estimate fully their effects. For purposes of this discussion, we define three major types of measurement effects. The first category, which we will call anomic, applies to instances when the formally stated rules for recording and classifying incidents are not followed by those who must implement them or when the rules do not prescribe a uniform procedure that can be unambiguously applied. The second type refers to designed variablility in practice resulting from the cost-error calculations of introducing such variability. The third category involves variability resulting from correctly applying formal rules that do not yield uniform results due to societal changes external to the data collection system.

Although both the NCS and UCR permit some discretion in the recording and classification of events, the amount of discretion permitted in the NCS is considerably less than that allowed police personnel in the UCR system. The Census Bureau employs more extensive and systematic procedures for limiting interviewer, coder, and editor discretion of its participants than does the UCR.[1] The relative emphasis on structuring discretion in the two systems is indicated by the amount of detail provided for in the basic instructional manuals. The *Uniform Crime Reporting Handbook* (FBI, 1980), which explains the procedures for classifying, scoring, and submitting data to the UCR, is 89 pages. The *NCS Interviewer Manual* (Census, 1987) contains 552 pages.

The Census Bureau reinterviews a sample of each month's respondents in order to check performance and to identify problem areas (Graham, 1976). Although numerous audits of state and local UCR programs have been conducted over the past 20 years, these audits are not done continuously or on a systematic sample of participating agencies.[2]

Largely because of the differences in the organization of the two systems we know a great deal more about nonuniformity of measurement

---

[1] For a discussion of some areas of discretion not routinely examined in the reinterview program see Biderman, 1981a.

[2] For a summary of 25 audits conducted by the International Association of Chiefs of Police, see the *IACP/UCR Audit/Evaluation Manual*, 1976. A study of the UCR system, by Abt Associates, as identified approximately 50 additional audits conducted in local police organizations (Poggio et al, 1983). Consequently, the effects of the use of discretion should be greater in the UCR system than they are in the NCS. The survey is also affected by the discretionary judgments of its staff, but the largest systematic errors in the survey are more often procedural errors (Biderman, Cantor, and Reiss, 1982; Biderman and Lynch, 1981; Reiss, 1982).

in the NCS than we do about measurement effects in the UCR. The survey is dedicated to the collection of statistical information whereas the major purpose of police departments is to provide police services to which the collection of crime statistics is at best ancillary and their provision to national system a by-product. The Census interviewers are selected, trained, paid and deployed exclusively for statistical purposes. The police personnel who provide information in the UCR rarely are. The Census is firmly enmeshed in disciplines of survey research and statistics, which encourage a certain degree of self-scrutiny and inquiry into measurement effects and methods for reducing them. All of these factors have encouraged a substantial amount of research to identify and measure procedural errors in the NCS quantitatively (Balvanz, 1979; Bushery, 1974, 1981a, 1981b; Bushery and Woltman, 1979; Cowan, 1976; Cowan, Murphy and Wiener, 1978; Dodge, 1975, 1979; Murphy and Dodge, 1981; Murphy and Cowan, 1976; Woltman, 1981; Turner, 1977; Singh, 1981; Woltman and Bushery, 1975). The UCR system does not have equivalently facilitating factors. Audits of individual departments have been conducted but these evaluations are fragmentary and by no means sufficient for estimating the magnitude and directional effects of sources of unreliability and invalidity in the UCR system as a whole. Consequently, our discussion will focus disproportionately on the NCS. In the very near future, however, with the implementation of the incident-based UCR, we will be able to say a great deal more about the error structure of that system.

Nonuniform Use of Discretion in the UCR

The transformation of a crime incident into a UCR report of offenses known to the police is a product of many decisions about the classification and scoring of the incident. The uniformity with which *UCR Handbook* definitions are applied in these decisions across departments and over time is highly questionable. The FBI acknowledges the wide range of factors affecting crimes reported in the UCR in the brief introduction to *Crime in the United States* titled "Crime Factors". We know from audits and other research on the UCR that considerable variation exists in classifying certain types of incidents.[3] Although quality control and edit procedures currently in place can identify and correct for some sources of this nonuniformity, other major sources are not attended to. The import-

---

[3] The "definition-by-example" format used in the *UCR Handbook* invites variability in classification. Examples can only cover a limited range of the behaviors eligible for inclusion in a particular class of crime. Therefore, the status of large components of eligible behavior are ambiguous and left to the discretion of the person classifying events.

ance of these disparities for the UCR series and NCS–UCR discrepencies has often been dismissed by assuming that they are either random, offsetting or otherwise in constant ratio to reported quantities over time. Although such assumptions are convenient, they are not well supported by available data. We must know considerably more about the nature and magnitude of nonuniformity in the application of UCR rules before we can have confidence in the UCR series or proceed with the investigation of sources of divergence.

Sources of Nonuniformity in the Application of UCR Rules

Since the inception of the UCR, approximately 50 audits have been undertaken to evaluate the quality of the information provided by a local police department. More recently, the Abt study of the UCR (Abt Associates, 1984) explored UCR data quality through interviews with representatives of 42 state programs and 19 local or county police departments. Although none of these investigations can be used for national estimates of the magnitude of measurement effects, they do provide a partial catalogue of major sources of nonuniformity in the UCR.

The Abt study (Poggio, 1983) identified six types of departures from currently prescribed UCR procedure. We modified this classification somewhat to fit more easily into a discussion of the discrepancy of the NCS and UCR. The modified typology includes:

1. *Classification and scoring issues.* Participants do not employ UCR criteria for including incidents in Return A; they apply classification rules incorrectly such that an incident included in the UCR statistics is included under the wrong type of crime category; they misapply offense counting rules.
2. *Poor record-keeping and transcription errors.* Participating agencies at the local level fail to complete or to maintain adequately records describing incidents, thereby precluding evaluation of the eligibility of the incidents for the UCR and the accuracy with which they have been classified and counted.
3. *Errors in addition.* In systems employing summary tally forms, participants sometimes inaccurately add the total number of reports before sending the summary report on to the FBI or the state UCR program.
4. *Duplicate reporting.* In incident-based systems, participants can mistakenly include two or more reports of the same incident. Another form of duplication occurs when two or more departments separately count the same incident.
5. *Downgrading and upgrading.* These are special cases of a classification and scoring error in which participants intentionally employ definitions of eligibility and classification rules making an incident eligible or eli-

gible for the UCR Index or to make it a more or less serious crime within the Index. This is generally done to affect perceptions of agency performance or of the crime problems it faces.

6. *Nonreporting.* By formal or informal policy, a participating police department may specify that certain types of NCS-eligible crimes should not be the subject of a formal report and will therefore not be included in the UCR system. A second type of nonreporting occurs when a police departments fails to submit its report for one or more reporting periods. The UCR program adjusts for this error by imputing missing data, but the imputation process itself has not been publicly evaluated and may introduce error.

In addition to listing general types of error, the Abt study assembled some illustrations of types of crimes particularly susceptible to error. Aggravated assault, for example, is especially problematic because state statutes and local custom involve standards such as degree of injury or weapons use that are at variance with those of the UCR. Larceny was also a problem because of the high number of incidents that are formally eligible for counting as larcenies but which involve little monetary loss. Practice varies widely with regard to treating minor larcenies formally or as *de minimis* incidents.

The Abt study is useful in that it assembles conveniently a great deal of previously known information. It also illuminates a few areas not heretofore documented—notably, the imputation procedures employed by the FBI. It provides little information on the magnitude and direction of the problems it identified, however. We would need to know, for example, how often participating agencies apply too stringent, as opposed to overly inclusive, standards of injury in classifying aggravated assault. How often are minor larcenies not reported? What is the frequency of duplicate reporting? These data and other information are required before we can begin to estimate the effects of nonuniform applications of UCR definitions and procedures on change in the UCR Index offenses known to the police.

Interactions With Social Change

As we have previously indicated, it is conceivable that annual-level estimates in the UCR could be seriously affected by nonuniform application of definitions and procedures without having any significant effect on the adequacy of the UCR as a measure of change in crime reported to the police. In other words, if the magnitude and direction of the net effects of nonuniformity each year are in constant or nearly constant ratio to the Index over time, then they will be of no importance to the major uses of the aggregate Index series. All of the information currently available, however, suggests that the UCR system, the police system on which it depends and the society that the police serve have all changed in ways that have caused and will cause sources of nonuniformity to vary systematically over time. Some of that variability is the result of the laudable efforts of the BJS, the FBI, the International Association of Chiefs of Police (IACP), and others to improve the UCR system. In the last 20 years, a number of changes have occurred that should have substantially reduced some of the sources of nonuniformity identified earlier. Increases in the number of state programs from only one in 1967 to 42 in 1986, as well as the increase in the number of states with mandatory reporting statutes, have reduced the amount of nonreporting due to nonparticipation. In the period 1973 to 1986, the number of agencies participating in the UCR system has doubled and the proportion of the U.S. population covered has increased by more than 6%. The growth in state programs and the increased use of incident-based systems as opposed to summary-based systems should have reduced the number of addition errors, the amount of missing data, and the number of duplicate reports in UCR data. The quality of data presumably has some positive relation to the length of a participating agency's experience with the program. The remedial training provided by the state programs should also help reduce those classification and scoring errors resulting from ignorance of UCR definitions and procedures. If these improvements have been at all successful, and there is at least anecdotal evidence that they have been, then it is difficult to assume that the sources of nonuniformity to which these improvements were directed have remained constant. Furthermore, as the system continues to improve, it is unlikely that such an assumption will be warranted for some time to come.

During this period of radical change in the UCR system, the American police system was also undergoing changes that lead us to have questions about how constant are the effects of procedural errors, ambiguities and nonuniformities on the UCR Index series. Since the mid-1960s, there has been a growing demand for greater efficiency and equity in the delivery of police services. The police responded by organizing police departments in a more bureaucratic fashion (Walker, 1977). Administrators attempted to increase their control over field personnel through more detailed record systems and high-technology information processing. Police personnel became more specialized and citizen demands for service were segmented and matched with those specialists regarded as best equipped to handle them. As part of this increase in specialization, civilian employees were introduced into police departments in unprecedented numbers to reduce the costs of providing police services. All of these efforts to increase efficiency have repercussions for classification and scoring of offenses for UCR purposes. Specifically, we have argued that these changes have discouraged the use of police discretion in the definition and classification of some citizen complaints with the result that over time more complaints ultimately become reports entered into the UCR system (Biderman,

1967: 125–127; Lynch, 1983). The increases in efficiency resulting from these organizational and technological changes have systematically reduced the pressures leading local departments to avoid reporting or to downgrade incidents.

Police administrators have attempted to increase their control over field-division personnel by requiring more information on their activities, by synthesizing this information with the assistance of Automated Data Processing (ADP) and other high-technology aids, and by incorporating this information into routine administrative reviews (Colton, 1972). Although much of this information was used to obtain more efficient allocation of patrol resources, it also made more of the patrol officers' behavior visible to supervisors, including the discretionary judgments the officers exercised in defining and classifying events. This is not to say that the discretion of patrol officers was eliminated, but rather that field division personnel felt more compelled to "paper" their decisions and, thereby, gave formal treatment to events that were heretofore treated informally. We hypothesize that the effects of formality would be particularly pertinent for reducing the nonreporting of minor larcenies noted in the Abt report.

In the past 20 years, police administrators have also begun to limit the number of functions performed by any staff member in the belief that specialization encourages the development of expertise and facilitates evaluation of personnel. Specialization also permits greater differentiation among personnel such that many functions performed by highly trained and expensive sworn personnel could be performed by cheaper civilian staff. The creation of civilian specialties within police departments is particularly consequential for classification and scoring in the UCR because dispatch and recording functions, which are so important for defining and classifying complaints, are increasingly performed by civilians. McCleary, Bienstadt and Erven (1982) have shown that civilian dispatchers are much less likely than sworn personnel to screen out complaints on the basis of their discretionary judgments. Whereas the "street cop" ethos encourages, even demands, the use of discretion, the more bureaucratic orientation of civilians and their ancillary status, coupled with their lack of police experience, discourages discretionary judgments. Because civilian dispatchers screen out fewer calls for service, more incidents become eligible for inclusion in police records and ultimately the UCR.

In addition to differentiating their staff into specialties, police administrators began to segment demand for service in order to fit the specializations they had instituted. Attempts were made to identify those calls for service that required the judgment of police officers and that would most likely lead to arrests and recovery of stolen property (Police Executive Research Forum, 1981; Chicago Tribune, 1983). Patrol officers are dispatched to these incidents, while whole classes of incidents that require

TABLE 3.1. Percent of departments using or projecting computer use by year and jurisdiction size.

Jurisdiction size	Year		
	1971[a]	1974[b]	1983[c]
500,000 or more	100.0	100.0	100.0
	(20)	(20)	(19)
250,000 to 499,999	79.3	89.3	100.0
	(29)	(29)	(29)
50,000 to 249,999	35.7	63.1	100.0[d]
	(252)	(252)	(71)
All departments	38.8	52.5	100.0
	(376)	(376)	(119)

[a] Respondents indicated that they used computers at the time of the survey (Colton, 1972).
[b] Respondents indicated that they planned to use computers by 1974 (Colton, 1972).
[c] Respondents indicated that they used computers at the time of the survey. Note that this survey is not as exhaustive or systematic as those for 1971 and 1974. The overlap between the surveys is substantial for departments in jurisdictions of 250,000 or more but much less for smaller jurisdictions. Consequently, 1981 estimates for smaller jurisdictions may be high (PERF, 1981).
[d] The PERF survey did not include departments in jurisdictions under 75,000 population. This category includes departments serving jurisdictions between 75,000 and 250,000 population. Because larger departments are more likely than smaller departments to use computers, this estimate of computer use is probably high.

less "street" experience or have a low probability of arrest are handled by civilians on the phone. When officers were sent to investigate every complaint, there was a great deal more pressure not to take reports on relatively minor incidents. With segmentation of demand more reports are taken and thereby become eligible for inclusion in the UCR.

There is good evidence that all of these changes in police organizations have swept through the American police system in the past two decades. There is also some evidence that these changes have contributed to a steady decrease in the level of downgrading and nonreporting in local police departments participating in the UCR. The proportion of all police departments using some form of ADP has increased steadily throughout the past 20 years (see Table 3.1). The use of civilian personnel and the segmentation of demand into in-person and telephone or other less intensive forms of service provision have also increased steadily (see Table 3.2).

These changes in police organizations were not uniform across all types of jurisdictions during the period, however. Large jurisdictions were the first to adopt some strategies beginning in the late 1960s and continuing apace through the early 1970s by which time the bureaucratic patterns had become firmly institutionalized in many larger jurisdictions. The rate of organizational change in these jurisdictions therefore slowed in the period 1976 to 1981. During the period 1973 to 1981, the increase

TABLE 3.2. Civilian employees as a percent of all police department personnel by year and type of jurisdiction.[a]

Jurisdiction type	Years		
	1973 to 1976	1984 to 1986	Percent change
1,000,000 or more	14.2	17.9[b]	26.2
500,000 to 999,999	17.4	20.1	15.0
250,000 to 499,999	17.4	23.5	35.2
100,000 to 249,999	18.0	22.3	23.9
50,000 to 99,999	16.7	20.8	23.9
25,000 to 49,999	14.6	19.5	33.3

[a] These data were computed from FBI, *Crime in the United States* 1973 to 1986, Table 58.
[b] This percentage is based upon data reported for 1985 and 1986. The data for 1984 were not used because one of the larger agencies was excluded from the report between 1981 and 1984. This amounted to a 20% change in the number of agencies in the largest size category. This resulted in a sharp increase in the percent civilian between 1980 and 1981 and a sharp decrease in that figure between 1984 and 1985. Although there is attrition in all size-of-place categories over time, the number of agencies in the largest place category is so small that any attrition is consequential. For this reason 1984 was omitted from the analysis.

in the appearance of these organizational changes was most pronounced among moderate-sized departments, that is, those with populations of 25,000 to 500,000. Smaller jurisdictions began adopting them in the 1980s.

The differential rates at which the changes occurred in various types of jurisdictions provide an opportunity for a rough test of the assertion that they reduced the amount of nonreporting or downgrading of offenses. We would expect that nonreporting and incident downgrading would have originally been greater in the moderate-sized departments than in the larger ones. UCR rates, therefore, would be expected to become progressively higher with organizational modernization. In order to control for increases in the pool of crime events potentially capturable by police reporting systems, Lynch (1983) computed a reporting rate that was the ratio of the UCR burglary rate in these jurisdictions to the NCS rate of burglaries reported to the police. If our assertions about the effects of organizational changes on nonreporting and downgrading are correct, then we would expect this ratio and the organizational changes described above to increase steadily for the moderate sized jurisdictions and not to increase as steadily for the largest and smallest jurisdictions. As can be seen in Figure 3.1, this indeed proved to be the case.

Change in Population Composition

Demands on the police were also shifting during the period 1973 to 1986 because of dramatic changes that were taking place in the composition of the population, particularly, changes associated with the maturation of the "baby-boom bulge." During the 1970s, these population dynamics

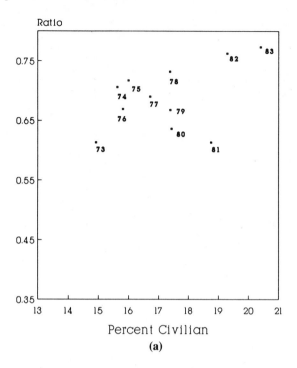

(a)

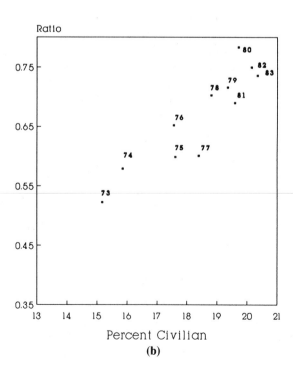

(b)

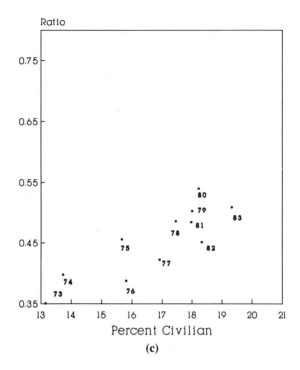

FIGURE 3.1. (a) Places over 500,000 population: for the largest class of jurisdiction, the ratio of UCR burglaries to NCS burglaries known to the police does not increase uniformly with the increases over time in the proportion of civilian police employees. (b) Places 25,000 to 500,000 population: in medium-sized places, this ratio has a strong positive relationship to the growing proportion of civilian police employees throughout the period 1973 to 1983. (c) Places less than 25,000 population: in the smallest jurisdictions, there is a weak positive relationship between the ratio and the increasing proportion of civilian employees.

were most pronounced within the narrow youthful age span in which the probabilities of victimization are highest. Within this range, the distributions of age and educational attainment were shifting upward. The NCS informs us that upward shifts of each of these variables is associated with more complete reporting of victimization to the police and thereby with higher UCR rates (Biderman, Lynch and Peterson, 1983). Moreover, studies of the use of police discretion suggest that these same factors encourage more formal treatment of citizen complaints and, therefore, less nonreporting and downgrading in the UCR (Black, 1970, 1980; Block and Block, 1980; Reiss, 1970; Sykes and Clark, 1980; Wiley and Hudik, 1980). In the eighties, these population dynamics were reversed in part and this contributed to reductions in UCR Index rates.

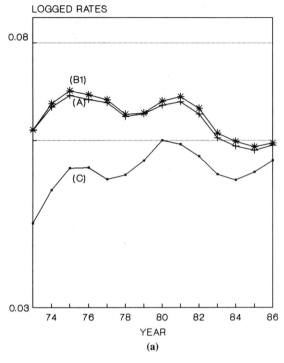

(a)

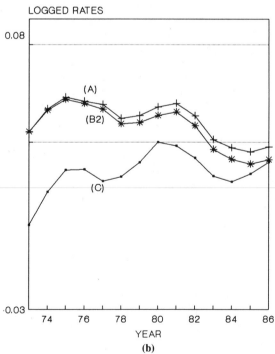

(b)

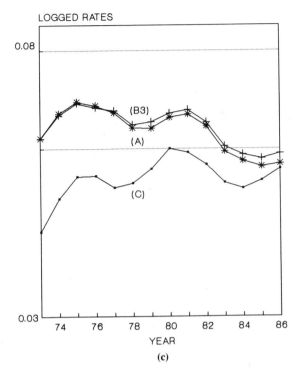

LOGGED RATES

FIGURE 3.2. NCS victimization rates (A) for index crimes reported to the police are estimated assuming no change after 1973 in the proportions of interviews conducted (B1) bounded; (B2) with household respondents; and (B3) both bounded and with household respondents. Actual victimization rates for bounded and unbounded interviews and for household and secondary respondents are used for each year. The bounding adjustments slightly reduce the discrepency between annual changes in the NCS and the UCR (C), while the household respondent adjustment increases the convergence of the trends.

   The greatest difference in reporting to the police is that between persons of high school age or younger and those above 20 years of age. According to the NCS in 1973, 32% of incidents involving teenage victims came to be known to the police, as compared with 50% of the incidents involving young adults (20 to 34) and 57% of those with older adult victims (35+) (Bureau of Justice Statistics, 1973). In the early years of the NCS, the teenage component of the population was still growing, although the average age within that group was at a minimum at the very first year of the survey. In the mid-1970s, the tail of the bulge had reached that range and the teenage component was growing much less rapidly than the young adult population, so that there was progressively a lessening of the babyboomers' negative influence on the overall police reporting ratio.

After 1980, the teenage component of the population declined even more rapidly than in the 1970s, the young adult population also began to decline, and it was the more mature age range that began to grow as a proportion of the total population. The effects on rate changes of the two series from this set of population dynamics were greater from the reduction of victimization with maturation than from the differential police reporting of victimization at various ages.

This set of age dynamics also affected the proportion of crimes reported to the police that were ultimately recorded for UCR purposes. To the extent that the police are more likely to treat formally crimes reported by older rather than younger persons, the aging of the "baby boom" resulted in increases in UCR rates without necessarily an increase in UCR-eligible complaints. This effect was probably greatest in the 1970s when "baby boomers" were young enough to have high levels of victimization, but becoming older such that more of their victimization experience was reported and recorded.

The NCS informs us that reporting to the police is also related to the educational attainment of victims.[4] Only 27% of the Index crimes involving persons with less than a high-school education are reported to the police, whereas 36% of those involving high-school graduates, and 35% of those including college graduates are reported (BJS, 1973). During the 1970s, levels of educational attainment of the population increased markedly. High school noncompletion rates fell more than one percent a year for cohorts that reached age-eligibility for the NCS during the 1970s. As a presumable consequence, progressively more of the victimization people experienced was reported to the police. Again, to the extent that the police treat more formally complaints by higher as opposed to lower status persons, then increases in the educational attainment of the population will result in a greater proportion of these complaints being recorded in the UCR. The rate of increase in educational attainment diminished and the average attainment actually decreased from 1985 to 1987. This change should have led to a decrease in the UCR relative to the NCS in the period 1981 to 1986.

The foregoing discussions are more suggestive than definitive, but they do call into question the assumption that error is constant across time and jurisdictions. If the continuous efforts to improve the UCR undertaken in the last 30 years have been at all successful, the consequences for the data could well have been systematically directional to a greater extent than they were mutually negating or random. Most of these changes have been in the direction of gaining more exhaustive recording of incidents and

---

[4] The higher reporting of high-school than college-educated population components is due to lower proportions of college graduates in the very high-reporting older-age population.

toward reducing interjurisdictional procedural variation and errors in the application of the definitions and rules of the UCR. Moreover, major changes in the police institution have undoubtedly affected the character of the data submitted to the UCR. We presented some evidence that the consequences of these improvements also were systematic, making less tenable the randomness and constancy assumptions.

Procedural Sources of Nonuniformity in the NCS

The NCS design involves a host of procedural components. It is known that the choice of different design alternatives will make for major differences in the data. Elaborately controlled implementation is also required to prevent extraneous data variation. The survey apparatus, however, is less than perfect in insuring uniformity of treatment across all units of observation and across time. There are not only variations in treatment, but also what is formally uniform treatment can be different in effect when applied in variable circumstances. Most of the procedural components of the NCS have been chosen after some consideration of cost-and-error trade-offs for level estimates. To date, however, the effects on the series of many of the sources of variability have yet to be treated in the literature on the survey.

Identifying Major Procedural Sources of Nonuniformity

The Crime Survey Research Consortium (CSRC) and the Census Bureau have invested considerable time and effort toward identifying sources of major measurement effects and toward estimating the direction and magnitude of these effects. Particularly important problems were the following:

1. *Recency bias.* The current NCS asks respondents to recount eligible victimizations they have experienced during the preceding 6 months (i.e., the six calendar months prior to the month in which the interview takes place). When the distribution of reported victimizations is plotted by the month in which they were said to have occurred, more than twice the number of victimizations are found in the month proximate to the date of interview as in the temporally most remote month. The most common explanations for this distribution are (1) a typical forgetting curve, in which failure to report an event becomes more likely with the passage of time, or (2) "telescoping" of time resulting in misdating of events so that more incidents are shifted back in time so that they fall outside of the reference period than are shifted forward into it (Bushery and Woltman, 1979).

2. *"Bounding" effects.* The NCS employs a longitudinal panel design in its samples of seven successive interviews of each panel at 6-month intervals. A key reason for adopting this design was the finding in methodological pretesting for the NCS that indicated a pronounced tendency for respondents to report incidents as having occurred within the 6-month reference period that actually occurred prior to it, that is, "telescoping-in." In dealing with similar problems encountered in panel surveys on other topics, the Census Bureau employed a panel design. This design was presumed to control this behavior by "bounding" the data so that each interview provided a temporal bound for data collected at the next one. Because of the magnitudes of the effects attributed to "telescoping," employing this control was regarded as critically important. Consequently, the NCS sought to avoid use of "unbounded" data for published incidence estimates. It implemented the control by excluding data from interviews in housing units that are in sample for the first time. The occupants of housing units change over time, however, and the first interviews for new occupants of previously sampled households are accepted for data despite their being "unbounded." Similarly, where an individual or an entire household was not interviewed successfully at first time in sample, data from a successful interview at a later time in sample is accepted. Because such first interviews are used for data purposes, they presumably contribute to a large overestimate of victimization (Biderman, 1981c; Biderman, Cantor, and Reiss; 1982). Biderman and Cantor (1984) estimate that about 18% of the interviews contributing to NCS estimates in the 1970s were first ("unbounded") interviews and that the failure to bound increased the number of victimizations used for published estimates by almost 50%.

3. *Household and respondent effects.* In order to save interviewer time and reduce the number of duplicate reports of the same events, the NCS asks only one respondent in each household to report "household crimes," namely, burglary, theft of household property, and motor vehicle theft. All members of the household (or surrogates for members ages 12 and 13) are asked about personal crimes such as rape, robbery, and aggravated and simple assault. Studies of the effect of respondent status on reporting have found that respondents report far more personal victimizations when interviewed as household respondents than the same persons do when interviewed as secondary respondents. Some of this increase in reporting is due to the allocation of incidents classed as "personal thefts without contact" solely to the first member of the household who reports that incident. That person is usually the household respondent. Another plausible source of the high rate for household respondents is the more extensive questioning they receive relative to other members of the household. Allocating personal thefts to household respondents has no effect on aggregate

TABLE 3.3. Household size, respondent status, and average number of age-eligible respondents per household in the NCS by year.

Year	Household size[a] (% with one person)	Average number[b] of person 12+ per household	Respondent status[c] (% household respondents)
1973	19.7	2.33	43.6
1974	20.4	2.29	44.1
1975	20.8	2.28	44.7
1976	21.1	2.29	44.5
1977	21.5	2.27	45.2
1978	21.8	2.25	45.5
1979	22.5	2.24	45.9
1980	22.9	2.22	46.3
1981	23.1	2.21	46.6
1982	23.3	2.21	46.8
1983	23.7	2.19	47.0
1984	24.0	2.18	47.6
1985	24.1	2.17	47.9
1986	24.1	2.17	48.2

[a] These proportions were obtained by manipulating the data on NCS public use tapes, variables v1030 (household members 12 years of age and older) and v1031 (household members under 12 years of age).
[b] Source: *Criminal Victimization in the United States*, Table 1.
[c] The proportion of interviews conducted with household respondents was determined from the NCS public use tapes using variables v2006 (peron line #) and v1015 (line # of Household respondent).

rates generated by such incidents, in that it merely shifts the attribution of an incident from one to some other member of a household. The more extensive cuing received by household respondents, however, could have had a biasing effect on the series. The probability that victmizations will be recounted increases as the average size of household in the nation decreases. This is because the proportion of all respondents interviewed as household respondents increased (Biderman, Cantor and Reiss, 1982).

4. *Proxy effects.* The NCS permits a proxy respondent for a household member (1) 12 or 13 years old, or (2) temporarily absent, or (3) physically or mentally unable to answer questions. The primary source of proxy interviews is the 12- and 13-year old group. The use of proxy interviews for self-respondents has been shown to result in underreporting of victimization in the NCS (Reiss, 1982).

5. *Time-in-sample bias.* Analysis of NCS data has demonstrated that victimization rates vary inversely with the number of prior interviews a respondent has experienced. The reasons for this decline in reporting are not well understood. A favored, though purely speculative ex-

planation is decline in respondent motivation—"respondent fatigue," loss of interest, accumulation of burden. A more specific motivational speculation is that respondents learn to avoid the burden that reporting victimization brings. Persons who give positive answers to screen questions learn that they are subjected to the burden of detailed questions about the incident. As a result, these respondents may be reluctant to court this burden again by reporting victimizations in subsequent interviews (Lehnen and Reiss, 1978). Biderman and Cantor (1984) also explain time-in-sample bias in terms of learning, but they suggest that the exposure to detailed questioning about the incident communicates to the respondent the cruciality of accuracy and thereby reduces loose and expressive incident mentions in subsequent interviews. These various explanations for the time-in-sample effect have very different implications for the quality of NCS data. If the various burden arguments are correct, then time-in-sample bias contributes to under reporting. If respondents are learning to report more accurately, then time-in-sample bias may reflect relative over reporting in initial as opposed to subsequent interviews.

6. *Telephone Interviewing Effects.* The proportion of interviews conducted by phone has increased substantially since 1973 when virtually all of the NCS interviews were conducted in-person. The increase was particularly dramatic in 1980 and 1981. This shift in the mode of interviewing may have affected the reporting of crime incidents in the survey. There is some evidence in the general survey literature, however, that telephone and in-person interviews do not yield very different results (Groves and Kahn, 1979). With respect to victimization surveys specifically, studies done outside of the Census Bureau indicate that personal visit interviews and a random digit dialing telephone interviewing procedure produced essentially similar estimates of victimization rates (Klecka and Tuchfarber, 1978). This evidence was obtained by investigators with an apparent stake in telephone interviewing and RDD and it comes from surveys with designs very different from the NCS. There is, therefore, some question as to whether this evidence is applicable to the NCS. Experiments contrasting maximum use of telephone and in-person interviewing in the NCS indicate that maximizing the use of telephone interviewing results in fewer reports of crimes than does a maximum personal visit strategy or the mix of in-person and telephone currently used in the NCS (Woltman and Bushery, 1977). The increased telephone use in the NCS is not exactly the same as the maximum telephone strategy evaluated in the experiment. Consequently, it is unclear whether the results of this study can be extended to the increase in telephone usage occurring in the survey over time. Quasi-experiments have been conducted to evaluate specifically the effects on reporting of the dramatic increases in telephone interviewing that took place in February of 1981 (Sliwa and Roman, 1982a). This evaluation indicated that the increase in telephone

interviewing did not substantially affect rates. There was some debate about the methodological adequacy of this study, however, and we cannot rule out some effect on the rates due to the increase in telephone interviewing (Roman and Sliwa, 1982a, 1982b).

There are other sources of known and suspected rate-affecting nonuniformities of procedure in the NCS survey (see Appendix B), but the above are the sources of the most consequential effects that have been documented.

Some effects are more consequential than others for year-to-year change measures. Recency bias, for example, should not vary very much over time as long as the 6-month recounting period is employed because recency bias has been shown to be only moderately related to characteristics of incidents or respondents (Biderman and Lynch, 1981). Proxy respondent effects seriously distort data for 12- and 13-year-olds, and can have affected rates as the last of the "baby boom" generation passed beyond that range. Except for the effects of the initial interview, additional repeat interview are found to have only slight effect on the number of incidents recounted (Biderman and Cantor, 1984).

The household respondent and first-interview effects appear to be the two most consequential sources of nonuniformity in the survey and they create the greatest potential extraneous influence on the measures of change. We know that household respondents report substantially more personal crime than secondary respondents do (Biderman, Cantor and Reiss, 1982), and that this effect seems to hold even when other important differences between household respondents and other respondents are controlled statistically (LaVange and Folsom, 1984). Moreover, as mentioned earlier, we know that during the 1970s and 1980s, the average size of households in the United States became smaller with more persons residing in one- or two-person households in 1986 than in 1973. As a result, a progressively greater proportion of the NCS sample are household respondents. The increases range between 0.2% and 0.7% per year (Table 3.3).

In addition to increasing the proportion of respondents receiving the cues of the household respondent screen, the net new formations of households makes for a slight increase of rates because of the way in which NCS counts household crimes and no-contact larcenies. Incidents of these two classes that occur during the portion of the reference period when the respondent was a member of some other household are attributed to the current household. After the division of a two-person household into two one-person households, for instance, both members would be eligible at their new locations to report a burglary at their former home during the reference period.

Although declines in the number of respondents per household have the effect of increasing aggregate victimization rates by exposing a higher proportion of respondents to the more extensive cues that household respondents receive relative to secondary respondents, Biderman, Cantor and Reiss (1982) identify an offsetting procedural consequence of decreasing size of households. For incidents that more than one respondent may report, the chance that an incident will not be reported at all in a household will vary with the number of persons contributing to the data taken in that household. An incident that one member of the household forgets to mention in his or her interview may be mentioned by some other member of the household in theirs. Members of households also may be present at each other's interviews and informal observations suggest that they often remind each other of reportable events that have not been mentioned. The NCS forms make specific provision for going back to complete incidents reports when a later respondent in a household mentions an assaultive incident that an earlier interviewed member should have reported but did not. That many heads are better than one for producing comprehensive recall at least partially offsets the aggregate rate-increasing consequences of declining sizes of households discussed above.[5]

Particularly striking is the high frequency with which victimizations are mentioned in "unbounded" interviews, that is, interviews with respondents who were not interviewed at the previous time their panel was contacted. On average, these first interviews yield incidents at twice the rate of "bounded" ones. (Biderman and Cantor, 1984). Again, multivariate main effects models of NCS rates have shown that the partial effect of bounding is substantial (La Vange and Folsom, 1984).

Some interviews were "unbounded" because the interview for the previous reference period was not successfully completed. In the main, however, the "unbounded" interviews were with respondents who had recently moved into sample housing units. Bounding status in the NCS, therefore, is a function of the mobility rates of the population.

In work by the Census Bureau on "bounding" effects, households were treated as a unit in defining the term "bounded" so that an interview was considered bounded if any member of the respondent's household had been interviewed at the previous time in sample. Most of the interviews treated as "unbounded" in Census Bureau data on bounding, including some which we use here, involve members of "replacement households," that is, households new to the sampled location.

Household mobility rates have varied historically with major economic and demographic developments. For instance, the recessions in 1974 and

---

[5] Data from the Victim Risk Supplement (VRS) tells us that interviews conducted in situations of company are not rare. Approximately 29% of all interviews in the VRS were administered in the presence of persons in addition to the respondent. In 8% of all interviews Census staff indicated that these persons contributed information during the interview.

TABLE 3.4. Bounding status of interviewed
households in the NCS sample by year.

Year	Percent unbounded[a] households
1973	12.6
1974	11.6
1975	11.1
1976	11.5
1977	11.7
1978	11.9
1979	12.3
1980	11.2
1981	11.1
1982	10.7
1983	11.0
1984	11.0
1985	11.5
1986	12.0

[a] "Unbounded" in this table means that no interview was conducted with a household respondent from this household the last time that this housing unit was in sample. This does not include "unbounded" interviews with members of households in which a household respondent was identified the previous time that the unit was in sample. The proportion of "unbounded" households was obtained by manipulating the NCS public use tapes variable v1022 (household status).

1981 each temporarily reduced mobility and, therefore, the proportion of interviews that were conducted unbounded. Table 3.4 suggests that the proportion of unbounded households decreased during the 1973 to 1975 recession during the weak recovery from 1976 to 1979, and fell again at the start of the second recession in 1980. The occurrence of unbounded interviews remained low until the recovery in 1984 to 1985, when it began to increase again. Variability in the proportion of interviews that are unbounded can also affect year-to-year changes in NCS rates by lowering rates during times of low mobility and increasing rates in periods of high mobility. Changes range from 0.3 to 1.1 percentage points in a year. Part of the mobility involves the formation and dissolution of households, which is responsible for the change in the ratio of household respondents to all respondents mentioned above.

The great variation of mobility rates with age is a particularly important consideration when the effects of "bounding" on the time series are at issue. Mobility rates are at a maximum for ages 20 to 24—ages at which victimization rates are high. Mobility falls off monotonically from ages 25 to 29 onward. For persons 65 and over, the rate is a small fraction of that for the young adult category. Teenagers, who have higher victimization rates than the young adults, have much lower mobility rates. Given that (1) "bounding" effects are critically dependent on mobility, (2) mobility varies greatly with age, and (3) the specific age variation of mobility rates is closely related to the age distribution of victimization rates, the change in the age distribution associated with passage of the baby boom bulge again becomes highly relevant. The relationships are too complex for analysis with the limited data that were available on mobility during the 1970s.

For full evaluation of the effect of these historically varying influences upon this key measurement effect of the NCS, it is important to consider it in relation to other changes in the demographic composition and social organization of the population. By adjusting the NCS annual estimates for these changes, we will be able to assess in an aggregate fashion how much they contribute to the differences observed between the paths of the two series.

Effects of Nonuniform Measurement on NCS and UCR Divergence

Our assessment of the effects of nonuniform measurements on the discrepancy of the NCS and UCR series involves two stages. In the first stage, we standardize the series for the effects of known and estimated measurement effects. In the second stage, we examine whether adjustments we can apply for these effects increase the degree to which the two time series correspond to each other. Given the paucity of useful data on effects in the UCR, all of the adjustments will be made to the NCS data. This process will take as its starting point the trends presented in Chapter 2, that is, trends adjusted for known and estimable differences in definitions and procedures in the two systems.

Standardizing the NCS Series

The adjustments to the NCS made here are quite simple ones.[6] The 1973 NCS is chosen as a reference point or a standard of uniformity. Thus, for the years following 1973, the body of interviews contributing data for each year is made to have the same proportionate distribution as in 1973 of data from the following methodologically relevant interviewee categories: (1) household respondents who are bounded (HRB), (2) household respondents who are unbounded (HRNB), (3) secondary respondents

---

[6] More elaborate adjustment procedures have been explored by LaVange and Folsom, 1984.

who are bounded (SRB), and (4) secondary respondents who are unbounded (SRNB). The adjusted level estimate for each year of the series
is computed using the following equation:

$$E_J = \sum_{i=1}^{N} (R_{ij} * P_{i73}),$$

where R_{ij} is the reported victimization rate for the ith procedure group in
the jth year, and P_{i73} is the percent of the sample in the ith procedure
group for 1973.

This procedure does not purport to adjust for error; it corrects only for
nonuniform applications of procedures over time. Consequently, we need
not and do not maintain that the procedures used or rates reported in
1973 are more correct than those of other years, but simply that this
initial year of the NCS is being employed as constant standard. We also
make the assumption that there were no significant interactions between
survey treatments and other rate-affecting variables over time. If, for
example, household respondent status interacts with age such that the
difference between rates for younger HR and older HR is greater than
the differences between younger SR and older SR, then this standardization will not be adequate. During the period 1973 to 1986, the age
composition of the HR became progressively younger so that if there had
been an interaction between age and respondent status, our procedure
would have proved to have been too conservative. Although we know
that age and other variables are related systematically to bounding and
respondent status, we do not know whether there are interactions that
affect reporting. More work like that of LaVange and Folsom (1984)
cited earlier, will provide more information on this point. For now,
however, there is no reason to assume that interactions between treatments and other major rate-affecting variables have an effect on the NCS
series.

By allowing group-specific rates to vary over time, we avoid overadjust-
ments that would correct for actual as opposed to procedurally induced
changes in reported victimization rates. We know, for example, that
increases in the proportion of household respondents will occur as the
prevalence of single-person households increases, as well as of plural-
person but single-respondent households. It has also been suggested that
single-person households can exercise less guardianship and therefore
experience higher victimization rates (Cohen and Cantor, 1981; Cohen,
Kluegel, and Land, 1981). Increases in rates due to changes in household-
respondent status are procedural, whereas the rate increases are not
procedural to the extent that they are due to such results of the increase
in single-respondent households as reductions in guardianship. The latter
should not be held constant. By allowing the aggregate HR rate to vary
over time in our standardized model, we permit the rate for the HR
group to reflect the influence of the increasing proportions of single-

respondent households in the make-up of the group. Given our earlier assumptions about interactions between procedural and substantive factors, this method should allow the standardized series to reflect most actual changes in the rates while procedural effects are being held constant.

Similar standardizations were made separately for bounding status and for respondent status, using the following equation:

$$E_j = \sum_{i=1}^{N} (B_{ij} * P_{i73}),$$

where B_{ij} is the reported victimization rate for the ith procedure group defined by bounding status in the jth year, and P_{i73} is the percent of the sample in the ith procedure group for 1973; and

$$E_j = \sum_{i=1}^{N} (H_{ij} * P_{i73}),$$

where H_{ij} is the reported victimization for the ith procedure group defined by respondent status in the jth year and P_{i73} the percent in 1973.

NCS yearly estimates do change somewhat when variability in procedures is held constant, although the series retains its basic form. The series standardized only for bounding status includes annual rates that are higher than those reported in the unstandardized series, but the degree to which rates are higher is not constant across all years. The effects observed in 1975 and 1980 are much greater than those for other years. Holding respondent status constant produces annual rates that are lower than those of the unstandardized series but the differences between the standardized and unstandardized rates increase steadily over time. When we hold constant both bounding and respondent status, the series becomes less regular. The increases observed from 1973 to 1975 and from 1979 to 1980 stand out as do the decreases observed in 1976 to 1978. These observations suggest that some of the constancy in the NCS series is due to the interaction of measurement procedures with demographic and social changes that muted variation in the series.

The foregoing standardizations appear to have remarkably little effect on the NCS annual rates. The largest difference between NCS unadjusted and adjusted rates is 5.26%, with an average change in annual rates across all adjustments of 1.79%. The NCS and UCR indicators that receive greatest public and policy attention are not the annual levels, however, but rather the percent change in rate each system reports each year, as well as comparisons of the most recent percentage change in the rate with that reported the preceeding year or the mean annual percentage change for some previous period of years. Even very small changes in annual level estimates, can have a very substantial effects on the percent change from year to year. It may be more appropriate, then, to express effects of standardization on year-to-year change estimates as a percent change in the percent change. Expressed in these terms, the effects of the holding constant the proportion of respondents receiving specific proce-

TABLE 3.5. Differences between standardized and unstandardized rates for Index crimes expressed as percent of annual estimates and percent of change estimates.

	NCS standardized for					
	Respondent status		Bounding status		Bounding and respondent status	
		Percent difference between				
Year	Rates[a]	Rate[b] changes	Rates	Rate changes	Rates	Rate changes
1974	0.60	6.5	−1.31	14.4	−0.55	6.1
1975	1.00	8.5	−1.9	12.4	−.6	2.2
1976	1.06	3.8	−1.87	1.5	−.6	1.8
1977	2.11	80.0	−1.05	61.4	.8	117.8
1978	2.34	3.9	−0.9	3.9	1.37	8.5
1979	2.92	52.9	−0.26	56.7	2.5	109.7
1980	3.49	16.8	−1.68	40.3	1.7	24.8
1981	3.66	10.6	−2.0	20.2	1.97	16.8
1982	3.98	6.1	−2.4	8.6	1.58	7.3
1983	4.05	18.1	−1.9	10.8	2.0	17.4
1984	4.65	29.9	−1.94	8.7	2.65	29.2
1985	5.0	22.4	−1.37	33.7	3.32	42.1
1986	5.26	13.5	−.79	28.2	4.16	42.9

[a] This is the difference between the adjusted and the unadjusted rates expressed as a percent of the unadjusted rate.
[b] This the annual percent change in the adjusted rates expressed as a proportion of the change in unadjusted rates.

dures do not appear at all inconsequential (Table 3.5). The largest effect on the percentage change in rates occurs between 1980 and 1981 when bounding status is held constant. In that instance, the percent change of the adjusted rates is 118 percent of the change in the unstandardized rates. The average effect shown in the table is a 22.5% change in the estimate of percent change.

   As was discussed at the outset, this work was occasioned by contention involving comparisons of recent percent changes being reported by UCR for its most recent Index with those being reported by BJS for the NCS. Our next step, therefore, is to examine how comparisons of change in the NCS with that in the UCR are affected by the adjustments we have applied to the NCS.

Comparing the Adjusted NCS With the UCR

We will employ sums of squared differences to assess the effects of the adjustments to the NCS on its correspondence to the UCR series. Specifically, squared differences (SSD) are computed between (1) the expected annual percent changes in the UCR (1973 to 1986) that would be predicted from the percent change in the NCS for the same period and (2) the percent change actually observed in the UCR rates. Then we examine the degree to which the SSD is decreased or increased when the predicted changes are based on an adjusted NCS series, rather than the official one.

In these comparisons, the UCR series is adjusted, as it was in the previous chapter, for rate base differences with the NCS and for the inclusion of those classes of commercial crimes which are excluded from the NCS (Biderman, Lynch, and Peterson, 1983). The base for the UCR rate was made comparable with that of the NCS—namely, the noninstitutionalized population 12 years of age and older. Intercensal adjustments were also applied to the 1973 to 1979 base values as determined from 1980 Census results. Commercial crimes that are identifiable in the UCR, for example, nonresidential burglary, shoplifting, theft from coin machines, and bank robberies, were excluded from the numerator of the UCR rates.

The NCS was standardized for household-respondent status and for bounding status, as described in the previous section.

According to the SSD criterion, holding constant the proportion of household respondent status and the joint distribution of respondent status and bounding status in the NCS series lessens the correspondence of the changes in the two series (Table 3.6).[7] The bounding adjustment, however, does increase their correspondence.

Although it is somewhat surprising that such a small adjustments to the NCS series should have so great an effect, it is understandable that bounding adjustments improve the fit and household respondent adjustments do not. Standardizations of the NCS series will increase the correspondence of the two series if the factors held constant affect the NCS in

---

[7] The sum of squared differences (SSD) for percent changes in the NCS restricted to incidents reported to the police and the UCR with the numerator and denominator adjustments described in Chapter 2 is somewhat lower in Table 2.10 (178) than it is here (213). The NCS rates used in Chapter 2 were taken largely from *Criminal Victimization in the United States* (BJS, 1975–88). The rates used in this table were produced with the public use tapes available at ICPSR. In some cases, we were not able to reproduce exactly the published rates. In other cases missing data on whether the incident was reported to the police, bounding status or household respondent data required for our models contributed to differences between the rates used here and those in official reports. Including cases with missing data in the unmodelled NCS estimates and excluding them from the estimates based on models using bounding and household respondent status could affect the relative size of the SSD for modeled and unmodeled data. Differences between the modeled and unmodeled data should reflect the influence of the differences in survey procedure not missing data. For these reasons, we tolerated a disjuncture between the SSD analyses in Chapters 2 and 3 and used the rates computed with the data from the public use tapes that had all of the data necessary for modeling purposes. This should not affect comparisons made within Chapter 3.

TABLE 3.6. Sum of squared differences between (a) annual percentage change for the UCR adjusted for rate base differences and commercial crimes and (b) annual percent change of the NCS rate for crimes reported to the police standardized for changes in bounding and respondent status.

Comparisons	Sum of squared differences	Cumulative percent change in SSD
UCR adjusted and NCS reported to police	213.0	0
UCR adjusted and NCS reported to police adjusted for household respondent status	243.0	14.1
UCR adjusted and NCS reported to the police adjusted for household respondent status and bounding	228.6	7.3
UCR adjusted and NCS reported to the police adjusted for bounding	204.0	−4.2

ways that are systematically contrary to their effects on the UCR. Bounding satisfies these conditions, whereas changes in household respondent status do not. The business cycle affects both residential mobility and crime, and residential mobility, in turn, determines the rate of unbounded interviews in the NCS. During the economic slumps, the crime rates of both the NCS and the UCR increased and residential mobility declined. With the decrease in mobility, there came to be fewer unbounded interviews in the NCS, with a resulting negative influence upon NCS level estimates, including the estimates of crimes known to the police that are used in our comparisons. Holding constant changes in bounding status in this way makes for more consistent movements of the two series during economic slumps.

Other adjustments for changes in the proportion of household respondents or proxy interviews are dependent on less routine demographic changes and may be appropriate at some times and not others. The 12 to 13-year age category contributes a fairly high victimization rate to the NCS, but because of the proxy interviewing effect discussed earlier, that rate is less than what it would be if "properly" measured; that is, if this group's interviewing treatment was no different than other age groups.' Crimes involving these young victims usually involve equally young offenders and are often are not called to the attention of police or, when they are, are often handled informally and do not figure in UCR reports. If adjustments were made for the proxy respondent effect during a period such as the time of writing when the baby-boom echo has begun to expand the 12 to 13-year category, it would tend to increase, rather than decrease the discrepancies. It would do so, that is, unless adjustments also could be made for UCR's selective registration of what might (or might not) be encompassed in some definition of of the "true" universe of crimes.

Although quite speculative, the foregoing considerations suggest how the interaction of procedures and sociodemographic changes affects the utility of application of adjustments to the published series.

Conclusion

This chapter began at the point where Chapter 2 left off. We explored, as best we could with the data available, the degree to which nonuniform application of definitions and procedures in each system affected the correspondence of the two series as measures of year-to-year changes in crime. This analysis is preliminary in that redesign work on both series continues to yield bases for evaluating the effects on the series of inconsistent and ambiguous definitions and of nonuniform and defective procedures.

Our analysis suggests that such adjustments as we are able to make for intertemporal variation in major procedural nonuniformities of the NCS do not greatly affect the annual estimates of levels of incidents. They did have appreciable effect on estimates of annual percentage change, however. Because the both indexes change by a modest percentage in a given year, even small changes in annual level estimates can have a considerable effect on change.

Nonuniformity in the application of procedures will vary with major social and demographic changes. Useful adjustments were also made for changes in the proportion of interviews used for data despite their being unbounded. It is likely that the variation in the two series with social and economic change will make such adjustments informative as long as the NCS continues its current nonuniform interviewing practices. On the other hand, during the period we analyzed, standardizing for increases in the proportion of interviews that were conducted with household respondents lowered the NCS rates and made for greater departures of the NCS from the UCR. The increase of one-respondent households was due to a rapid rate of new household formations. This develeopment and correlated social changes were driving up the UCR rate during the period.

Comparison of the indicators yielded by the UCR and NCS must not be done mechanically or unthinkingly but rather with as much understanding as can be mustered regarding the interactions between the definitions and procedures of a statistical program and major social changes. A more comprehensive taxonomy of sources of variability of measurement, their interactions with social and demographic changes and their probable effects would be a useful guide, both to those who fret about the apparent conflict between the two systems and for those who want to understand why they differ.

In addition, this exercise reaffirms that the major obstacle to better understanding of differences between the two indicators is the paucity of knowledge regarding how the UCR is implemented at all levels from the person taking the original incident report on the street or in the station house on up. Both systems, but particularly the UCR, can be greatly improved by redesign to reduce the ambiguities of definition and non-uniformities in their application, as well as by building self-monitoring and self-correcting provisions in to the systems. For our present investigation, we have had to rely upon the data of the NCS to render that series more comparable to the UCR. That is because, in incomparably greater measure than the UCR, the NCS has levels of data disaggregation, specificity and documentation, explication of definitions and procedures, and established evaluative mechanisms. The research program for the redesign of the UCR has increased our grasp of the actual scope of the UCR of recent years and the accuracy, reliability and validity of its data, although many basic and important questions remain unanswered. Once the UCR redesign has been fully implemented, some of these questions will be mooted, but far from all.

In conclusion, a reminder is in order. The effort we are expending here on maximizing the commonalities of the NCS and the UCR should not obscure a basic point. The value of having the two systems resides far less in their likeness than in their distinctiveness with respect to scope, methods, auspices and results.

4
Summary and Conclusions

The preparation of this monograph was occasioned by comment in the press that the Uniform Crime Reports Index and the National Crime Survey presented conflicting information on trends in crime during the 1970s. The impressions, drawn from published aggregate rates, were that the UCR was suggesting sharp increases in crime while the NCS was showing decreases or no appreciable change. A similar situation reoccurred in the mid-1980s.

Apparent contradictions between the depictions of crime trends by the UCR and the NCS threatened the credibility of both programs. The editorial pages of the "prestige press" tended to see the discrepancies as confirmation of a critical view toward the UCR that they had long propounded. The NCS had been successfully introduced and vigorously defended as a "better indicator," free of such distorting influences as changes in public cooperation with the police or police reactions to recurrent exposes of police "killing crime on the books." The news columns of the same newspapers, however, tended almost invariably to report the periodic releases of each series uncritically, as did broadcast journalism. A result was the periodic resurfacing of the tension between the two systems.

Fruitless, repetitious, debates about which indicator is "better" have continued long after some basic points no longer should have needed demonstration. By 1974 (if not by 1967 with the President's Commission report of that year), victimization surveys had established and gained general acceptance of the point that the UCR failed to reflect a great many criminal events that were not being reported to or by the police. By 1976, if not by 1967, it was also established that using the victimization survey for national crime indicators was a complex, difficult and costly undertaking and that many conceptual and methodological problems were involved that remained to be satisfactorily solved. By the early 1980s, matters had progressed. Both systems had undergone extensive evaluations and were in the process of major redesign. Nonetheless, they retained the burden of meeting conceptions of both press and public that both should reveal accurately how much crime there was in the nation and whether there was getting to be more or less of it. When the two major series are seen as giving contradictory signals, it has almost universally been concluded that (at least) one of the two indices must be seriously in error.

The official, and scientific, explanation, to be sure, is that the two systems are bound to differ to a greater or lesser degree. As explained by the Bureau of Justice Statistics,

the portraits of crime from NCS and UCR differ because they serve different purposes and are based on different sources. (1983: 6; 1988:11)

The explanation, however, is regarded as of small help by the reporter who seeks "a number" to show how much more crime there "really" is (although having two indicators from which to choose has sometimes been convenient for the political incumbent who has wished to show how much more crime there "really" wasn't).

Furthermore, DOJ has always been uncomfortable with the possibility of having conflict between two national indicators, both of which purport to provide general barometers of whether the crime problem is worsening or lessening. From the outset, decisions of the agency regarding the programs have often been inconsistent with the concept of two measuring systems differently constituted and serving different purposes. In setting the original scope of the NCS, BJS's Justice Department predecessor sought to come as close as possible to the UCR Index. This decision lost sight of the criteria originally followed in selecting the offenses that would make up the UCR Index, namely, that the offenses included should be (1) serious, (2) common, and (3) regularly reported to the police. The last of these criteria is not only irrelevant but actually counterproductive for survey-based statistics on crime. For a survey measure, the appropriate counterpart to the "regularly reported to the police" criterion would be the likelihood that the type of offense would be regularly reported to survey interviewers. Indeed, the importance of covering a type of serious and common event by the survey would be proportionate to the likelihood that it would not be regularly reported to the police.

Similarly, the original designers of the NCS operationalized its basic offense definitions and they adopted units and counting rules to produce aggregate rates as similar as possible to those of the UCR. Many of the UCR elements that the NCS emulated had taken the form they did in the UCR because of the capabilities of police agencies—more particularly, because of the limitations of the agencies and, most particularly, because of the limitations of the smallest agencies least well equipped for applying elaborate rules and procedures for classification, counting and reporting. The original NCS design bent the survey form out of shape to accommodate to the UCR and, in the process, gave insufficient priority to employing concepts and procedures that most readily fit the survey method and the usefulness of the survey product.

Official documents also were prone to ignore or to explain away even radical differences between the NCS and the UCR. For example, BJS's 1983 *Report to the Nation on Crime and Justice* (p. 13) proclaimed in bold type: "NCS data confirm UCR findings about where crime occurs." The statement was true as far as it went, but the text and tables chosen were far from indicating how radically different the NCS and UCR distributions of crime rates by size of place actually were. NCS rates (multiples of the UCR rates for all categories of places) have only a fraction of the variation by type of area that the UCR displays. The NCS variation by type of place is also far less consistent than the UCR's; for example, the suburbs of central cities with populations 1 million or over average higher NCS rates for crimes of theft than do their central cities. The 1983 BJS report displayed only the UCR data in comprehensive form, selecting only the one type of NCS crime with the most radical (and UCR-like) variation by place for quantitative discussion. The corresponding section of the BJS's 1988 *Report to the Nation* (p. 19) showed more of the data of both series and made no comment whatsoever comparing the NCS and UCR distributions.

For many years (see Biderman *et al.*, 1967: 161–176), we have seen a need for liberating the NCS from the more costly burdens of aping the UCR Index so that it could more freely pursue the neglected potential that the victimization survey method possesses for informing the public regarding the crime problem. More recently, with a restructured UCR in the offing, it may be important that the simple consistency or inconsistency of the UCR Index changes with the aggregate change measures of the NCS should not be a criterion for judging the success of the redesign. This is not to say that achieving greater comparability as well as complementarity of the data of the two systems is not of great value. What we wish to forego is unduly costly pursuit of an annual chimerical number, the Index, for a numerical chimera, the "total amount of crime in the United States."

It should be clear that the present work in not an exercise at glossing over NCS–UCR differences and certainly not for Panglossing them. We have shown that the two series would and should produce rate changes that did not always coincide even if (1) both the NCS and UCR were free from errors of design and execution, which is decidedly not the case; (2) even if they made their definitions, rate bases, and counting rules as consistent as possible, which certainly is not now the case; and (3) even if one removed from consideration all crime events not falling in that core which is eligible for counting by both systems and which is accessible by both.

In order to promote an understanding of sources of divergence of the NCS from the UCR, we began with a comparison of the definitions and procedures used in each system and identified areas where differences could and did lead to discrepancies in annual change measures. Similar, but less detailed attention was given to nonuniformities in measurement within the two systems. These analyses provided valuable information about why changes in annual rates diverged during 1970s and a better understanding of the behavior of the two indicators during the period 1973 to 1986. More importantly, this work suggested ways in which these two systems could be revised for greater complementarity and for increasing the light they shed on the crime problem.

Understanding Discrepancies Between the NCS and UCR

When the comparisons between the two series were confined to those components of each that can be identified as dealing with a common universe of events, when the same units were used for crime counts and when rates for the two series were calculated on an equivalent population base, the two indicators displayed the same directional changes, with regard to both the general trend over the fourteen years and fluctuations from year to year. With only two minor exceptions, the points of inflection and the direction of change at these points were the same for the equated component rates of the two series. NCS–UCR differences in the magnitudes of rate changes and the general levels of crime also were greatly reduced. The trends for the two series converged rather than diverged over the period studied.

Reporting lags during the first decade of the NCS contributed to impressions of conflict with the UCR. The impressions were derived from the trend most recently reported by each series even though the most recently reported NCS dealt with earlier years than did the most recent UCR report. The reporting lags responsible for these erroneous comparisons were inherent in the rotational pattern and reference period features of the NCS design. The original reports on which the present volume is based recommended to BJS how collection-period data from the NCS could be used to achieve more timely NCS releases and thereby more contemporaneity of comparisons (see also Penick and Owens, 1976: 70–71). The NCS now rivals the UCR in timeliness by releasing preliminary annual estimates based on collection-period data.

Major remaining estimable sources of divergence of the unadjusted, aggregate series are as follows:

1. *Reporting to the police.* Over time, a larger proportion of all crimes falling within the NCS became crimes known to the police. This occurred because of declines in components of the population whose victimizations, in relatively high proportion, were not reported to the police, particularly the decline in the size of the youngest age groups.

2. *Comparability of rate bases.* The NCS treats large classes of crimes against households and publishes rates for these crimes on the base of households. In that the number of households increased much more rapidly than the number of persons in the population during the years 1973 to 1979, the NCS did not show increases displayed by the UCR. Translating the NCS series into a rate of incidents on the base of population brings it into much greater accord with the UCR. Because the NCS also excludes persons under 12 years of age—children who are included in the base of the UCR—the relative decline of this population component served to elevate UCR rates progressively rates relative to those of the NCS during the same period. Both of these population dynamics did not substantially affect discrepancies in the trends in the 1980s.

3. *Intercensal misestimation of the UCR base.* The UCR employed inter-censal estimates of the population for rates published from 1973 to 1979. The 1980 Census revealed that the growth of the population during these years had been underestimated. Part of the apparent increase in published UCR rates during the latter part of the 1970s is an artifact of its rate base becoming progressively underestimated. NCS rates were not similarly affected by these underestimates in that the weights applied to the crime counts of its numerator are equi-valently underestimated. Postcensal population adjustments, like those the FBI will apply after the 1990 census to revise its series for the 1980s, bring the UCR into closer accord with the NCS series.

4. *Commercial crimes in the UCR.* Only to a limited extent is it possible to identify those components of the UCR which involve crimes against businesses and other organizations that are not within the scope of the NCS. Analyses we were able to perform excluding commercial and organizational victimizations from the NCS–UCR comparisons did increase the fit of the two series over that obtained by the adjustments described above.

5. *Series crimes in the NCS.* Adjustments of NCS series to eliminate effects of procedures for the treatment of crimes occurring in a series of like events tended to increase slightly, rather than decrease, the divergences of the two series.

After all adjustments we could take to equate the two series were made, the NCS continued to yield estimates of crimes reported to the police that exceeded the UCR measure of crimes known to the police. This was true even of the one type of crime—motor vehicle theft—for which unadjusted UCR rates sometimes exceed those for police reported incidents in the NCS. UCR rates are universally lower than those for NCS police-reported motor vehicle theft when allowance is made for thefts of motor vehicles owned by businesses and other organizations.

That NCS estimates of police-reported crime substantially exceeded UCR rates indicates a margin exists for system improvements—whether it be a margin due to NCS overestimation or UCR undercounting.

Because crimes against commercial and business establishments cannot be completely identified in the UCR, it is currently impossible to identify fully the scope of property crimes common to both series. The problem is particularly severe for larceny—a crime class that contributes more than half of the crimes of the UCR Index. Most of the crimes in this UCR classification are ambiguous with regard to their eligibility for the NCS. UCR motor vehicle thefts are also ambiguous with regard to whether the vehicles stolen are household property, as is also the case with the property involved in many crimes in the burglary and robbery classifications. The changes proposed for the redesigned UCR will remedy this problem to a large extent, but the changes will not affect the data for the period studied here.

Although most of the obstacles to comparability during the period under study stem from informational limitations of the UCR, others are due to departures of NCS counting procedures from UCR rules. Most of the current problems of series comparability can be remedied by readily feasible design changes, but a few involve inherent differences in the requirements of the two systems. For example, some subpopulations contributing variably to the supply of victims and offenders elude the base of the UCR and others are not covered by the NCS. Even short-term changes can occur in the numbers of such persons—for example, sojourning foreigners, armed forces in barracks, and institutionalized persons—sufficient to produce divergences of the two series. The contribution of these population groups to the UCR numerator could be determined by revising the data that the UCR collects on the various statuses, for example, immigration status, of crime victims in the incident based UCR. Accommodating these populations in the base of the UCR rates, however, would require major revision and supplementation of our basic demographic statistical systems, since currently, we have no single data system that enumerates foreign visitors exhaustively. Moreover, the fundamental logic of the NCS sample would need to be altered to include the nonresidential population of the United States. Both systems are also subject to nonuniformities in measurement of appreciable magnitudes that may vary disproportionately over time. Some of these measurement effects are due to procedures such as the use of bounding interviews or household respondents that were developed to reduce the costs or improve the accuracy of a particular system. Changing these procedures to promote comparability could simply cause the return of the original problems.

Attention to all of the foregoing matters is not only important for insuring the compatibility of the UCR and the NCS as general indicators of changes in the level of crime, they are perhaps even more essential for making these statistics informative with regard to the nature and sources of change.

Implications for the Future of Crime Statistics in the U.S. The results of our analyses clearly establish that the differences in the social organization of the two data collection systems and the related differences in definitions and procedures are extremely important for understanding why the two series diverge. The contribution of these factors to understanding would undoubtedly be greater had it been possible to include the effects of other known but currently unmeasurable differences between the systems. Taking account of these differences in comparisons of the trends is not simple, however. A great deal more effort would be required to account completely for the effects of differences in the social organization of the two systems on how they would register change.

This raises the question of whether it makes sense to invest a great deal of effort in "reconciling" the patterns produced by such radically different data collection systems. Given the inherent differences between administrative record systems and household surveys, it may not be wise to attempt to make them measure the same things. The interest of both systems may be better served if priority were given to having each system measure that component of the crime problem that it measures best. In this way, the data from the two systems could be used in a complementary fashion, rather than a competitive one, to increase our understanding of the crime problem.

Comparability Versus Complementarity

The relative emphasis that should be given to comparability as opposed to complementarity of the NCS and UCR turns on our assumptions about the possibility of "objectively" identifying crime independently of the systems used to count it. If crime can be objectively defined and counted, then comparability may be a feasible goal to pursue. If not, then comparability should become less of a priority in maintaining and building the two systems.

On its face, the effort to identify crime objectively is a difficult one. While it may be possible to offer an agreed upon conceptual definition of crime, these definitions often cannot be operationalized easily. Subjective determinations are needed for identifying and counting events that should fall within any of many possible conceptual definitions of crime. For example, the conceptual definition of most crimes requires some judgments about the intent of the offender. Intent, in psychology if not law, involves an inference with regard to a subjective state and this inference process is not particulary reliable across persons and events.

In an effort to reduce the variability with which these determinations are made, rules are developed within statistical systems for determining what should and should not be considered crime. Although these rules are designed to increase the reliability of crime counts, they are unavoidably influenced by the social organization of the statistical system in which they will be used. Since the limitations of an administrative series such as the UCR are quite different from those of a household survey, the operational definitions of crime employed in each system necessarily differs.

Some components of the crime problem are operationalized comparably or "objectively" in both the NCS and the UCR, but substantial components are not. Since the major use of the two series involves measuring annual rate changes that are quite small, even limited amounts of "subjectivity" across systems can result in highly discrepant change measures.

The analyses presented in the previous chapters seem to support the contention that definitional and procedural differences in the data systems contribute substantially to discrepancies between the trends. When adjustments were made for many of the measurable differences in procedures and definitions across systems, the discrepancies between the series in both the level and change in level of crime were significantly reduced. Approximately 64% of the difference in relative annual changes between the series is accounted for by procedural and definitional dissimilarities. We are less able to assess the impact of nonuniformities in measurement on divergence, but it is clear that the two systems are affected by very different types of measurement problems.

Even with heroic efforts to identify and account for the effect of procedural and definitional differences between the two series, however, a substantial amount of discrepancy remains unexplained. As we noted above, some of this discrepancy may be due to those procedural differences or nonuniformities in measurement that cannot be assessed by any of our current means. Planned or conceivable changes in the two series, such as the more systematic identification of commercial crimes in the UCR, may increase the comparability that can be achieved. Reducing other sources of discrepancy would require extensive and costly revisions of both systems that are clearly beyond reasonable possibility. These extensive changes may gain comparability by incurring losses of other capabilities of the data systems. Even if all possible changes to the NCS and the UCR were made to make them absolutely similar in terms of procedures and definitions, and even if steps were taken to insure the uniform application of these definitions across systems, careful account would still have to be taken of any changes in society that might differentially affect the two series.

Given the difficulty of completely accounting for discrepancies between the two series, enhancing comparability may not always be the best way to exploit the potential these statistics have for illuminating crime problems. Better objectives for investments of time and money would be devoted to maximizing the unique contributions of which each kind of statistical system is capable. It may be more desirable simply to acknowledge that inherent differences in the NCS and the UCR make it inevitable that the two systems will diverge, quite apart from the results of any errors in their implementation.

Toward a More Complementary NCS and UCR

The complementary use of the NCS and UCR has been recommended in general terms for some time, but very specific suggestions as to how the systems could be changed or used to promote complementarity have not been forthcoming. We would advocate the following steps:

a. The idea should be abandoned that the NCS and UCR should aspire to as common a scope as possible. The crime statistics community should be encouraged to view the two series as related, but not congruent, in scope and concept. The example of employment statistics can be emulated. Employment and unemployment data are sought through an employer reporting system, counts of claims filed with state employment offices, and a household interviewing survey. They often move in different directions. Differences between the two indicators are regarded as sources of valuable inferences in themselves for understanding the economy, rather than as symptoms of embarrassing flaws in the measuring systems.

   Joint publication of NCS and UCR level and change estimates with a clear statement of this position might well contribute to changing public perceptions of the relationship between the two series.

b. The rationale for maintaining independent systems of crime incidence statistics should be less on their serving as checks on one another than on enabling each system to do that which it does best. To this end, NCS and UCR reports could give greater emphasis to reporting crime incidence for those components of the crime problem that are better measured by each and less attention to their overlapping areas. Currently, for example, the NCS affords much greater descriptive detail on individual crime events than does the UCR. The massive size of the UCR should be exploited for illuminating what are rare events for the NCS but all too common problems for the society, for example, assaults involving very serious injury. The NCS has a much greater capacity for varying its content to meet new interests than does the proliferate, cooperative UCR reporting system. The NCS, however, has been resistant to full use of its potential flexibility. Until full implementation of the UCR redesign, the NCS has incomparably greater capabilities for aggregating and disaggregating victimization data differently for different purposes and greater flexibility in pro-

ducing denominators for crime and incident rates. This capability
should be exploited more fully in published reports.

1. *Exploiting differences in scope.* Special attention in NCS reporting
   should be given to crimes not reported to the police. Similarly, the
   UCR includes commercial crime which the NCS cannot address.
   Commercial crimes should be given special emphasis in UCR reports, perhaps in an index of Crimes Against Business Property.
2. *Make fuller use of detail in the NCS.* Efforts should be made to
   develop new indicators of victimization that have greater congruence
   with public notions of risk than the do Index crimes.[1] For example,
   the concept of street crime as crimes involving strangers in public
   places cross-cuts several classes of Index offenses, but the level of
   street crime can be obscured when it is reported using current
   Index categories. Similarly enlightening would be disaggregation of
   the large and heterogeneous larceny category by the type of property taken. Some forms of theft are more or less important to the
   public and should be highlighted. These subclasses of larceny are
   not always captured by simple dollar-value distinctions. We have
   argued elsewhere that vehicle-related crime may be a useful classification given the unique and ubiquitous roles and special vulner-
   abilities of motor vehicles in our society.
3. *Using flexibility of NCS.* In some cases, the concept of risk is not
   individual, but collective. The victimization of a single person in a
   household affects all of its members. They all experience some
   increment of fear or some other reaction to the proximate experience of crime. Where this is the case a prevalence rate based on
   households would be a better indicator of risk than an incident rate
   based on individuals. Similarly, the standardization of change rates
   for changes in the composition of the population would help readers
   understand when changes in the level of victimization does not
   necessarily mean a change in risk for everyone. The NCS has the
   potential of following persons and households over time. This longitudinal capability of the NCS should be exploited more fully in
   BJS' routine reports.

c. NCS and UCR should be used to illuminate each other to a greater
   degree than they have been so used in joint reports such as *Report to
   the Nation on Crime and Justice* (BJS, 1985). Data from one series

---

[1] Some of BJS's special reports on topics such as stranger-to-stranger crime and
home intrusion have experimented with new crime classifications, but more can
be done. At minimum, these new classifications should be given greater prominence in general reports on the level and change in level of crime, rather than
being restricted to special reports that have more limited circulation.

could be used to explain or elaborate changes in the other. In some cases the two series can be used to test alternative explanations for changes in crime incidence. For example, the simple standardizations of rates for changes in the demographic composition of the population that we suggested above would help us understand why changes in incidence have occurred. It is important to know whether the changes are consistent with population change as opposed to new and unforseen social developments. Similarly, the two series could be used to determine whether a sudden increase in larceny is due to the theft of newly available consumer goods that are particularly attractive and ready targets, as new electronic gadgets in automobiles have regularly been or to new criminal opportunity structures, such as occurred with the simultaneous switch to self-service gasoline vending and the escalation of gasoline prices. While care should be taken not to promise too much "explanation," joint reports of NCS and UCR data could be used to assist users in understanding the changes in incidence statistics.

Currently, the greater detail and flexibility available in the NCS would make it more useful in illuminating the UCR than the reverse, but this may change with the implementation of the redesigned UCR.

d. More substantial gains in complementary utility can come from changes in the current systems that will allow each system to address those components of the crime problem that it is best equipped to address. The scope of the NCS, for example, should be expanded to include more crimes that are well reported in a self-report survey and are not as well reported in police record systems. In addition, the unique aspects of the organization of each system should be more fully exploited.

1. *Expanding the scope of the NCS.* In keeping with the rationale set forth here, the NCS Redesign research program proposed bringing several additional types of victimization into the scope of the NCS and it conducted some testing of the proposals. Most of these suggested expansions of scope have not been incorporated into the NCS redesign that has been implemented by BJS. Vandalism is the major exception, but even in this instance the implementation was compromised in the interests of not jeopardizing the continuity of the redesigned NCS with the old UCR-like rate series. Vandalism, by all indications, is a very common form of victimization and, as a class, it rivals larceny categories currently included in the NCS in seriousness of dollar loss. Other data suggest that the social importance of vandalism for processes such as neighborhood degeneration may be even greater than that of most larcenies.

An example of a suggested scope expansion that was not implemented by the NCS involved identifying whether victimizations were "Hate Crimes." Subsequently, legislation has required the

Justice Department to produce statistics on hate crimes.[2] A difficulty in determining if an offense is motivated by the kinds of hatred fitting the construct is that the intent must often be inferred from the community context in which it occurs rather than from anything manifest in the event itself. We have no reason to believe that these events would be more adequately reported to the police than they would be in a survey or that the police use of discretion in defining these crimes would be any better than a victim's judgment of the motive of the crime. Indeed, one could argue that the victim's perception of intent or motivation may well be socially more important than that of the police.

Another proposal suggested correcting a particularly egregious instance of the compromise of effective survey practice in the NCS by an effort to restrict its scope to the UCR Index classes. Since its first year, the NCS has oriented all of its screen questions dealing with assaults toward eliciting incidents fitting the UCR aggravated assault definition. The screen item dealing with threats of violence has included the phrase, "NOT including telephone threats. . . ." Not only does the NCS overly complicate its screen question, but the effort to conform NCS questioning about threats to the UCR definition of attempted aggravated assaults also enmeshes NCS instrumentation and reporting in illogical confusions between "attempts" and "threats" as crime concepts. The considerable pains it has gone through to exclude violence not fitting the UCR classes costs it the opportunity to illuminate the full range of violence and intimidation in the lives of Americans, including often terrifying and intimidating uses of the telephone.

2. *Modifying the organization of data collection.* Although it employs repeated interviewing of households impaneled for a three-year period, the NCS nonetheless has a cross-sectional logic in its crime data. It was designed to treat crime events as individual incidents at points of time without regard to any relation they might bear to other crime events experienced by the individual respondent or household. During the history of the NCS, there have been many attempts at surmounting these limitations of the design in analyses of its data. The efforts to link events to one another across time have entailed considerable effort, expense and hobbled product. There have been improvements in the database structure facilitating such uses of the NCS. The implementation of a truly longitudinal design, however, would vastly increase the ability of the survey to

---

[2] The Hate Crime Statistics Act of 1990 requires the collection of statistical data on "hate crimes."

address issues that require aggregation of crime events over time for persons or households.

Most of the modifications to the NCS suggested above would not involve costly changes to the survey. They would increase the time required to conduct interviews, but a marginal increase in the average time of the interview would entail a modest increment to survey costs. Indeed, it would seem more efficient to obtain more information from each person contacted once the more costly work of making contact with the respondent had been done.

Appendix A
Crime-Specific NCS–UCR Comparability Problems

Although the NCS was designed to yield data on the same types of crime as are included in the UCR Index, the two systems are far from congruent in scope. The specific classes of events they cover also are only partially equatable. Inherent differences between agency and survey statistics, as discussed for example by Biderman (1981a), as well as specific features of the NCS, make for differences in scope and classification.

Businesses, Households, and Persons

In the original planning by the Bureau of the Census and the LEAA for developing crime statistics by victimization surveys, the possibility of achieving exhaustive coverage of victimizing crimes was explored, including crimes of which both organizations and citizens in their private capacities were victims. The planners considered the feasibility of conducting surveys of victimizations of business organizations, government and transportation agencies, and farms, as well as a household survey. Only two of these surveys were ever implemented, a survey of commercial establishments drawn from the Census Bureau sampling frame and the household survey. In order to avoid double counting, provision was made for the Household Survey to exclude incidents that would be eligible for counting in the Commercial Survey (or any of the other organizational surveys then being contemplated). This provision has not been altered even though the Commercial Survey has long since been discontinued.

Accurate comparisons of the NCS and the UCR require distinguishing in the UCR between crimes against the property of individuals or their households and crimes involving the property of businesses or other formal organizations. In that the UCR does not attempt to make such a distinction consistently among property crimes, the extent of overlap of the two systems can only be imperfectly estimated. We will explore the gray areas that exist with respect to specific classes of crimes.

Property Crimes

For property crimes, including robberies, the UCR counting unit is defined as the distinct criminal operation, irrespective of the number of property holders victimized in that operation. The NCS makes no provision for identifying the number of victims in each property crime incident, with the following exceptions: (1) respondents reporting a robbery are asked to give the number of other persons robbed, assaulted or threatened in the same incident; (2) when an individual is harmed in a robbery of a business, the NCS records an assaultive victimization of the person, but no robbery incident; and (3) if an interviewer determines that two members of the same household are giving the same property incident, one of the multiple reports is voided. No known means are available for estimating the extent to which the NCS yields an overcount in UCR-equivalent units for larcenies and for burglaries in hotels, motels, lodging houses, and so forth which victimize more than one person. The UCR's "hotel rule" is to count only one offense for each such incident even when more than one guest or lodging quarters is victimized. and Plural victim "hotel-type" incidents have multiple chances of being represented in the survey and therefore are subject to overrepresentation in the NCS relative to the UCR.

Violent Crimes

By and large, the problems of NCS–UCR comparability are much less severe for crimes of violence than for property crimes. The NCS includes incidents of violent victimization even when the person is victimized while performing an organizational role, as, for example, assaults against law-enforcement officers or against a teacher by a student. The UCR also employs explicitly the concept of the individual victim as the counting unit for crimes of violence. One crime (offense, incident) is counted for each person murdered, raped, or assaulted. This counting method is equivalent to NCS victimization counts. (The NCS produces a count of violent-crime incidents essentially by dividing each victimization by the number of persons 12 years of age or over who the respondent says were also victimized in the same incident. The NCS in this respect produces an underestimate of the UCR rape and assault rates. For UCR-equivalence, the incident counts of the NCS for rape and assaults are irrelevant.)

Some special problems apply to the crime of robbery, which the UCR treats as it does property crime and the NCS treats as a personal crime. These problems will be discussed below.

Household Crimes

The UCR does not employ a distinction between "household" and "personal" crimes—a distinction of basic importance to both collection and classificatory procedures of the NCS. If one wishes to compare NCS rates for household crimes with corresponding UCR crimes, some problems also arise because of a lack of coherence to the household-crime category of the NCS. The basic needs of the survey entering into the concept were (1) certain crimes victimize all members, or at least some members of a household, collectively, and, therefore, (2) reports regarding these crimes could be gained economically by asking just one member of the household, rather than all members, about them. The household is taken as the victim unit for such crimes and victimization rates are tabulated on the base of households, rather than persons. As operationalized, however, questions asked only of one household respondent do not exclusively or exhaustively involve the element of collective victimization. The NCS household crime component becomes rather a combination of the categories of burglary—breaking and entering, motor-vehicle theft, and larcenies occurring at or immediately adjacent to the exclusive residential premises. For NCS–UCR comparisons, one may try to identify UCR crimes that largely coincide with NCS household crimes in definition and change the UCR base from a population of persons to a population of households. This has the advantage of showing how the more rapid growth of households than of persons has differentially affected NCS and UCR published rates. Alternatively, one can compute NCS household crime incident rates on a base of persons. This makes it possible to combine NCS household and personal crimes for comparison with the UCR where a household–person distinction cannot be applied to UCR data, or to use NCS data to construct rates equivalent to the UCR's total Crime Index.

Specific Crime Classes

The first step in NCS–UCR comparisons requires identifying, insofar as possible, the ares of common coverage of the two series, given differences in their operational definitions of types of crimes that are included in the UCR Index. We will discuss each of the UCR crime classes, in turn.

Homicide. The victim self-report rationale of the NCS precludes coverage of homicides so that this crime must be eliminated from the UCR Index for our present purposes.

Rape. The UCR definition of forcible rape is essentially the same as the NCS definition of rape. A major difference between the two series is that the NCS yields a much higher ratio of attempted to completed rapes (1979 = 4:7) than does the UCR (1979 = 1:3). Presumably, the police often apply more stringent criteria than do victims in judging what was a rape attempt, and a higher proportion of NCS completed than attempted rapes is reported to the police by the victim. The NCS does not present a definition of rape to victims and permits respondents to define the term as they understand it.

Robbery. The UCR treats robbery as it does property crime so that one offense (incident) is counted, regardless of the number of victims. The NCS treats robbery as a personal crime and counts a victimization for each person from whom property is taken in an incident where force or threat of force is employed. To facilitate comparisons with the UCR, the NCS forms an incident count by dividing each victimization by the number of other of-age persons in the encounter who were harmed, coerced, or lost property. Some error is associated with this procedure in that it assumes that all others victimized in an incident are as likely as the actual respondent to recall and report the incident. The probability that a victimization experience will be mentioned by a respondent varies with characteristics of the respondent and the interview (particularly, its recency). Any set of actually mentioned incidents disproportionately represents the higher-probability respondents and interviews. Underreporting factors would have to be introduced to reduce victimization counts to incident counts properly. This aspect of the NCS may be regarded as an error property beyond the scope of this book. The incident translation procedure also results in including among the victims some other persons, such as members of the armed forces living in barracks and sojourning foreigners, who are not in the NCS sampling frame. The latter error is doubtless of very small import for rates.

The major problem confronting robbery comparisons is that the UCR includes robberies where the property of businesses and other organizations is the target. As indicated above, the NCS includes robberies of organizations as victimizations (but not as incidents) when a respondent also loses personal or household property.

Identifying commercial and other organizational robberies included in the UCR requires using the UCR crime analysis data. Such data are provided on the Supplementary Form by reporting jurisdictions whose population totals do not coincide with those used by the FBI for computing the aggregate rates for each of the Index crimes. We do not know if the Supplementary Form data are selective in any way by type of jurisdiction.

The largest UCR subclass of robberies is "Highway Robbery." Some appreciable proportion of the highway robberies are directed at business property and would be ineligible for the NCS. Robberies of taxi and bus drivers, delivery persons, and street vendors are examples. We know of no data permitting estimation of this proportion for the national UCR. The same difficulty applies to a large UCR miscellaneous category, which includes victimizations in professional offices, schools, churches, wooded areas, airplanes, government buildings, and so forth.

The UCR Supplementary Form also includes several classes that, on their face, would appear to cover crimes against commercial organizations. In the 1980 Form, these categories were Commercial House, Gas or Service Station, Convenience Store, Bank. (In the earlier version in use during the period of our analysis, Chain Store rather than Convenience Store was included.) These categories identify the scene of the crime, rather than the victims, however. A robbery of patrons of a bar or gambling house, for example, would be classified properly as a Commercial House robbery, as would a case where one employee forcibly takes the property of another at a factory. If one excluded from comparison with the NCS those UCR robberies in such business locations, one would also have to exclude from the NCS the incidents occurring in such locations and in which no property belonging to the business was taken. The NCS collects the information required for doing this, and all robberies reported in the NCS as occurring in commercial establishments could be excluded from the NCS numerator for special analyses reported in this book.

Comparability with NCS also exists for the remaining category of the UCR, Residence Robbery. The current revision of the UCR *Handbook* (FBI, 1980) classifies robberies in hotels, motels, lodging houses and other transient accommodations as "Commercial House," however, and NCS place-of-offense codes would have to be employed to achieve comparability. Prior to 1980, the *Handbook* specified that robberies in motels —the only transient dwelling mentioned at all—should be classified as Residence Robberies. This may account for residence robbery constituting a much higher proportion of all NCS robberies known to the police than of the UCR total. In that the UCR total includes many commercial incidents, one would otherwise expect residence robbery to be a smaller proportion of the UCR class.

Aggravated Assault. The aggravated-assault category is probably the Index class with the greatest UCR-NCS definitional consistency. Differences would largely stem from the ways in which police and victims apply the criteria defining the crime. The NCS goes to great lengths to classify injuries and specific weapons to accord with definitions of "serious" employed by the UCR, so as to achieve separation of aggravated from simple assaults.

Burglary: Breaking and Entering. To the extent that the UCR Supplementary Form separates burglary into Residence and Nonresidence subclassifications, particularly high comparability should be possible for this class of crime. A counting complication exists, however, when several units of a hotel, or other multiple-unit lodging, are illegally entered "in the same operation." The UCR count for such events is one burglary, but the NCS affords no information for making a comparable adjustment of its incident count. It is not possible to identify the NCS burglary incidents in question (the NCS place code combines "vacation home" and "hotel/ motel" in the same category), nor can one identify the portion of the UCR Residence Burglary classification that is affected by the UCR's "hotel rule."

The NCS applies its burglary classification only to burglaries of victims' residences or of structures on the residential premises, as consistent with the Residence Burglary classification of the UCR. The NCS can record as larcenies some thefts of personal property in burglaries of nonresidential structures at which the respondent keeps property. Presumably, a frequent pattern in such instances would be for the victim to make a report to an authority of the establishment, rather than directly to the police. There would be no double offense count in the UCR, even where the establishment incurred no loss.

In that the NCS type-of-crime coding algorithm counts all assaults prior to burglaries, in those presumably infrequent instances where an illegal intruder inflicts a simple assault on a householder without taking property (i.e., no robbery), the NCS elevates simple assault in these instances over burglaries contrary to the UCR hierarchy. The survey affords the information necessary to identify these incidents and adjust the NCS rates accordingly.

Over six million burglaries are estimated by the NCS annually, however, and it would take a high number of minor assaults with forcible entry to have any substantial impact on the NCS burglary trends. If we take the most liberal indicator of forcible entry in the survey, that is, unauthorized presence of an offender in a dwelling, approximately 120,000 incidents involving both minor assault and forcible entry are estimated annually by the NCS on average. This is approximately 1.8% of the total number of burglaries each year—too small a component to have much effect on rate changes. Nonetheless, for completeness's sake this adjustment can be made.

Larceny: Theft. Thefts present a combination of UCR subclassifications that fall nicely within the scope of the NCS together with other subclasses for which no separation can be made between crimes against businesses and organizations and those against individuals and their households. The UCR Supplementary Form identifies pocketpicking and purse-snatching, which, with some rare exceptions, are comparable directly to the corresponding crimes of the NCS typology. Purse-snatching and pocketpicking are clearly single-victim crimes in both the NCS and the UCR. The NCS divides other larcenies into Household and Personal Crime categories by place of occurrence and no comparable distinction can be applied to UCR categories. It appears safe to assume that the property lost in such "from the person" incidents usually is not business property.

The UCR identifies bicycle thefts, which presumably also would be eligible almost universally as NCS incidents. Although the NCS instrument permits identifying bicycle thefts, unfortunately the NCS Public Use tapes available for our analyses do not provide a code category for this property item prior to 1979. Plausibly (we have not checked the data on this point), the use of force to take bicycles may not be rare, particularly among juveniles. Such incidents would be more likely to be identified as robberies in the NCS than in the UCR. In the direction of exclusion, the UCR identifies two classifications—Shoplifting and Thefts from Coin-Operated Machines—that are clearly commercial.

We are able, therefore, to sort 13% of the 1979 UCR thefts into clearly NCS-eligible categories (Purse-snatching and Pocketpicking—%; Bicycles—11%), and to exclude 12% (Shoplifting—11%; Coin Machines—1%). The remaining 76% of the 1979 UCR thefts is completely ambiguous with regard to the proportions that are crimes against businesses (From Motor Vehicles—17%; From Buildings—16%). Where analyses in this book have sought to exclude commercial crimes from the UCR, we have excluded the 12% of larcenies that are clearly ineligible and included the rest, unless otherwise indicated.

Additionally, we mentioned earlier the possible multiple-counting by NCS of larceny incidents involving property losses to more than one person.

Motor vehicle theft. The UCR and NCS definitions of motor-vehicle theft are in the main comparable. The NCS, however, has limited the definition of motor vehicles to those "legally allowed as a means a transportation on most roads and highways." The UCR *Handbook* (FBI, 1974) in use during most of the period in question provided for inclusion of other vehicles, listing specifically farm equipment, bulldozers, airplanes, and construction equipment. The illustration of airplanes in the *Handbook* is an inconsistency, in that the theft of an airplane is given as a specific illustration of an offense to be scored by the Larceny-Theft category, and the general definition given by the *Handbook* restricts the category to vehicles "that run on the surface." The 1980 *Handbook* explicitly excludes airplanes, farm equipment, construction equipment, and bulldozers. Its motor-vehicle definition still is somewhat broader than the NCS definition in that the former explicitly includes snowmobiles and, inferentially, other off-the-road vehicles such as trailbikes and golf-carts.

All motor-vehicle thefts are treated as Household Crimes by the NCS.

Within the UCR's motor-vehicle-theft data, thefts of business-owned and household-owned vehicles cannot be differentiated. Some rough estimates of the proportion of thefts in each category can be attempted from UCR Supplementary Form data on the types of vehicles stolen and data from other sources on the proportions of these types owned by households, if it is assumed that theft rates vary primarily by type of vehicle rather than by type of ownership.

We will use the year 1977 because survey data are available for that year on the types of vehicles owned by households (Motor Vehicle Manufacturer's Association, 1981). In that year, there were about 1.53 automobiles and trucks owned per household of which about 1 in 5 were trucks. Using these ownership rates, we multiplied the ownership rate times the number of households in 1977 to obtain an estimate of privately owned automobiles and trucks. The ratio of our estimate of privately owned automobiles and trucks to *total* registered trucks and automobiles provides an estimate that about 86% of the automobiles and 62% of trucks and buses were owned by households. In that year, there were about 112 million automobiles and 30.1 million trucks and buses registered (excluding government vehicles). In addition, there were about 4.9 million motorcycles and about 5 million tractors (exclusive of garden tractors) and other farm vehicles the UCR classed as vehicles for Index purposes (Bureau of the Census, 1981:622, 680). We can only guess at what proportions of these vehicles in the "other" categories are owned by households. In that we are dealing with a small percentage of vehicles and of thefts, we can proceed fairly safely with pure guesstimates. We will assume that about 90% of the motorcycles and 20% of farm and other miscellaneous vehicles are household owned.

The UCR crime analysis for 1977 divided motor-vehicle thefts as follows: automobiles—80%, trucks and buses—9%, and other vehicles—10%. If we assume thefts in proportion to ownership, we would estimate that 69% of the 1977 UCR thefts were household automobiles and 6% thefts of household-owned trucks or buses. Attributing a much higher theft rate to motorcycles than to farm and other vehicles, as found in a 1974 UCR special survey of motor vehicle theft (FBI, 1975: 37–39), we would estimate about 8% of the 1977 thefts were other vehicles owned by households. In sum, about 83% of the 1977 UCR motor-vehicle thefts are thus estimated to be thefts of household vehicles.

During the years covered by this monograph, thefts of automobiles (sometimes termed "passenger cars") represent a decreasing proportion of all motor vehicle thefts—1974, 85%, 1977, 80%; and 1981, 75%. This trend occurred despite the 1981 change in the *Handbook* restricting the miscellaneous types of vehicles included in the classification. We surmise that this trend is mainly or entirely due to the increased ownership by households of motorcycles, trucks and of recreational vehicles classified as trucks by the UCR *Handbook*, rather than to a shift toward proportionately more theft of business vehicles.

Appendix B
Some Sources of Measurement Variation in the National Crime Survey and Major Demographic Developments During the Decade of the Survey That May Have Affected Their Influence on the Data Series

Major demographic developments, 1973 to 1986:

A. changing population pyramid—maturation of the baby boom generation and the growth of the elderly population;
B. changing rate of new household formations and changing size of households (especially number of persons per household 12 years of age or over and eligible to be NCS respondents);
C. changing rate of geographic mobility of persons and households;
D. growth and decline of geographic areas and changes in prevalence of population in various forms of housing;
E. immigration.

Sources of Measurement Variation in the NCS

	Influential demographic development
Bounding interviews	
Whether or not R's household was interviewed at prior time in sample	B, C, D, E
Whether or not R was interviewed at prior time in sample	A, B, C, D, E
Scope of prior interview (e.g., whether or not incident report taken)	A, B
Interview status	
Whether R interviewed as designated household respondent or as secondary respondent, only (R's	

under 18 years of age, by rule, rarely designated as household respondent)	A, B

Interview mode

Personal visit or telephone	A, B, C, D, E

Proxy interviews

Proxy interviews almost universal for Rs 12 to 13 years of age	A
Proxy interviews for certain difficult-to-interview Rs	A, E

Intrahousehold respondent interactions and procedural rules

Preemptive procedures regarding R from whom incident report is taken and for designating one or more household members as victim in incident	B
Prompting of one R by another member of household—procedurally prescribed or spontaneous	B
Possible reticence of nonprivate interview	B

Panel effects (other than bounding)

Number and character of prior interviews completed, as they affect	A, B, C, D, E
attitudes toward interview and interviewer, selective panel retention, and information and understanding about interview purposes and demands	

Interview noncompletions

Type A (no interview completed in household)	B, E
Type Z (noncompletion for member of interviewed household)	A, B, E
Position of noncompletion(s) in panel sequence	?
Imputations for noninterviewers and weighting	C

Treatment of victimization reports as a series

Exclusion of series crimes from estimates and major tabulations	A
Variable treatment of reports as series or separate incidents by interviewer and respondents	A

Recency bias (temporal variation of incident recall)

Variation by characteristics of event, respondent and
  interview style
Variation by interval between end of reference period
  and interview date
Concentration of collection in first few days of month
  biases representation of holiday-related victimizations: "Never on Sunday" bias

Other systematic interviewer effects

Differences between data from experienced and in-
  experienced interviewers and differential ratios of
  old and new interviewers by time and place   C, D
Field office and supervisory dependent variables   C, D
Respondent—interviewer rapport with repeated
  contacts as related to interviewer and turnover   C, D

Cognitive demands and biases of instruments

Education and class-cultural variation in respondent
  understanding and application of concepts and
  cues   A, E
Sex bias and other stereotypes in questionnaire   A

Dependence of recall on reinforcement, novelty
balance

More ready recall of events with reinforcing seque-
  lae: e.g., with lasting injury, reported versus non-
  reported to police, for insured versus uninsured
  property   A
More ready reporting of nonroutine than routine
  victimizations   ?

Ambiguous, obscure, and difficult definitions and procedural rules

Whether or not definition or rule is incorporated
  in instrument, in manual, in memo, and stressed
  in training; regularity with which key concepts
  are or are not made explicit to Rs in course of
  questioning   ?
Ambiguous rules and definitions, e.g., "near home,"
  "use of motor vehicle as weapon"   D
"Gray area" victimizations and inherent ambiguities
  at bounds of concepts "crime" and "victim"; ab-
  sence of provisions for ascertaining legal or subjective crime status of participants' actions in
  incident   ?

Changes of questionnaire content and rules

(See Martin monograph.)

Changes in collection system

Add and cut sample	A, D, E
Increased use of telephone	B, C, D
Start-up panel imbalance	
Allocation of sample to tests and possible contamination by test procedures	A, C, E

Mobility into and out of sampling frame

Asymmetries of flow, e.g., immigration, military mobilizations and demobilizations and sea and foreign deployments; institutionalization and de-institutionalizations of offenders, mentally ill, and aged	A, C, D, E
Age asymmetries in flows	A, E

Counting of household crimes reported by respondents from merged or divided households

Household victimizations at prior household subject to double-counting probability	B

References

Abt Associates.
  1984 *Final Draft of Interim Report National UCR Conference.* Cambridge, MA: Abt Associates.

Balvanz, Bill A.
  1979 "The Effects of the National Survey of Crime Severity Supplement on Victimization Rates Determined from the National Crime Survey," Memorandum, U.S. Bureau of the Census, Washington, D.C., October 15, 1979.

Biderman, Albert D.
  1966 "Social Indicators and Goals." in Raymond Bauer (ed.) *Social Indicators.* Cambridge MA: MIT Press.
  1981a "Where Does the NCS Push the Baby Carriage? Victimization of Children and General Problems of NCS Procedure." Item 655 in SKGJ: CSRC [on-line teleconference]. Washington, DC: Bureau of Social Science Research.
  1981b "Sources of Data for Victimology." *Journal of Criminology and Criminal Law* 72:789–817.
  1981c "Dealing with Move In and Out of the NCS-Defined Population." Item 324 in SKGJ:LCSRC [on-line teleconference]. Washington, DC: Bureau of Social Science Research.

Biderman, Albert D., et al.
  1967 *Report on a Pilot Study in the District of Columbia on Victimization and Attitudes Toward Law Enforcement. Field Surveys I.* Washington, DC: U.S. Government Printing Office.

Biderman, Albert D. and David Cantor
  1984 "A Longitudinal Analysis of Bounding, Respondent Conditioning and Mobility as Sources of Panel Bias in the National Crime Survey." Paper presented to Annual Meetings of American Statistical Association, Philadelphia, PA.

Biderman, Albert D., David Cantor, and Albert J. Reiss, Jr.
  1982 "A Quasi-Experimental Analysis of Personal Victimization Reporting by Household Respondents in the NCS." Paper presented at the American Statistical Association Meetings, Toronto.

Biderman, Albert D. and James P. Lynch
  1981 "Recency Bias in Data on Self-Reported Victimization." Proceedings of

Social Statistics Section, 1981. Pp. 31–40. Washington, DC: American Statistical Association.

Biderman, Albert D., James P. Lynch, and James Peterson
1983 "Why the NCS Diverges from the UCR Index Trends." Paper presented at the American Society of Criminology, Denver, CO.

Black, Donald
1970 "Production of Crime Rates." *American Sociological Review* 35:733–748.
1980 *The Manners and Customs of the Police.* New York: Academic Press.

Block, C.R., and Block, R.L.
1984 "Crime definition, crime measurement and victim surveys." *Journal of Social Issues* 40:137–160.

Block, Richard, and Carolyn Rebecca Block
1980 Decisions and Data: The Transformation of Robbery Incidents into Official Robbery Statistics. Chicago, IL: Illinois Law Enforcement Commission.

Bureau of the Census.
1987 NCS Interviewer's Manual. Washington DC: U.S. Department of Commerce.
1972– *Statistical Abstract of the United States*, 1973–89. Washington, DC:
1988 U.S. Department of Commerce, Bureau of the Census.

Bureau of Justice Statistics
1985 *Blueprint for the Future of the Uniform Crime Reporting Program.* Washington, DC: U.S. Department of Justice.
1973– *Criminal Victimization in the United States*, 1973–1986. Washington,
1986 DC: U.S. Department of Justice.
1989 *Bureau of Justice Statistics Annual Report Fiscal*, 1988. Washington, DC: U.S. Department of Justice.

Bushery, John M.
1981a "Recall Biases for Different Reference Periods in the National Crime Survey," paper presented at American Statistical Association Annual Meeting.
1981b "Results of the NCS Reference Period Research Experiment," Memorandum, Washington, D.C.: U.S. Bureau of the Census, March 31, 1981.
1974 "Spurious Changes in Levels of Reported Crime in the NCS Sample Due to Time-in-Sample Bias and Number of Months of Recall," Memorandum for the record, Washington, D.C.: U.S. Bureau of the Census, November 27, 1974.

Bushery, John M. and Henry F. Woltman
1979 "Panel Bias and Length of Recall in the NCS," Memorandum for David V. Bateman, Statistical Methods Division, U.S. Bureau of the Census, Washington, D.C., May 16, 1979.

Chicago Tribune
1983 "New Police Chief Changes Strategy to Fight Crime." P. 1, Section 4, August 26.

Cohen, Lawrence, and David Cantor
1981 "Residential burglary in the United States: Lifestyle and demographic

factors associated with the probability of victimization." *Journal of Research in Crime and Delinquency* 18:113–127.

Cohen, Lawrence, and Kenneth Land
1984   "Discrepancies between crime reports and crime surveys: Urban and structural determinants." *Criminology* 22 (4):499–530.

Cohen, Lawrence, and M. Lichbach
1982   "Alternative measures of crime: a statistical evaluation." *Sociological Quarterly* 23: 253–266.

Cohen, Lawrence, James Kluegel, and Kenneth Land
1981   "Social inequality and predatory criminal victimization: An exposition and a test of formal theory." *American Sociological Review* 46:505–524.

Colton, Kent
1972   "Police and computers: Use, acceptance and impact of automation." *The Municipal Yearbook*, 1972. Washington, DC: International City Managers Association.

Cowan, Charles D.
1976   "Twelve to 13 Year Old Interviewing Experiment," Memorandum for Anthony G. Turner, Statistical Research Division, U.S. Bureau of the Census, Washington, D.C., April 8, 1976.

Cowan, Charles D., Linda R. Murphy, and Judy Wiener
1978   "Effects of Supplemental Questions on Victimization Estimates from the National Crime Survey," Paper presented at Annual Meeting of the American Statistical Assocation, August 14, 1978.

Decker, D.L., D. Shichor, and R.M. O'Brien
1982   *Urban Structure and Victimization*. Lexington, MA: Lexington Books.

Dodge, Richard W.
1975   "Series Victimizations: What is To Be Done?" Memorandum, Washington, D.C.: U.S. Bureau of the Census, October.
1979   "Proposed Research on Response Bias in the National Crime Survey," Memorandum, U.S. Bureau of the Census, Washington, D.C., April 1979.
1987   "Series Crimes: Report of a Field Test," Special Report, Bureau of Justice Statistics, Washington, D.C., April.

Ennis, Philip H.
1967   *Criminal Victimization in the United States: A Report of a National Survey*. (Field Surveys II). Report to President's Commission on Law Enforcement and Administration of Justice. Washington, DC: U.S. Government Printing Office.

Federal Bureau of Investigation
1974   *Uniform Crime Reporting Handbook*. Washington, DC: U.S. Department of Justice, The Federal Bureau of Investigation.
1980   *Uniform Crime Reporting Handbook*. Washington, DC: U.S. Department of Justice, The Federal Bureau of Investigation.
1982   *Uniform Crime Reporting Handbook*. Washington, DC: U.S. Department of Justice, The Federal Bureau of Investigation.
1973–   *Crime in the United States: Uniform Crime Reports*. Washington, DC:
1986   U.S. Department of Justice, The Federal Bureau of Investigation.

1988a *Uniform Crime Reporting National Incident-Based Reporting System: Data Collection Guidelines*. Washington, DC: Federal Bureau of Investigation.

1988b *Uniform Crime Reporting National Incident-Based Reporting System: Data Submission Specifications*. Washington, DC: Federal Bureau of Investigation.

1988c *Uniform Crime Reporting National Incident-Based Reporting System: Approaches to Implementing an Incident-Based Reporting System*. Washington, DC: Federal Bureau of Investigation.

1988d *The Redesigned Uniform Crime Reporting Program*. Washington, DC: Federal Bureau of Investigation.

Gove, Walter, Michael Hughes and Micheal Geerken
  1985 "Are Uniform Crime Reports a Valid Indicator of the Index Crimes? An Affirmative Answer with Minor Qualifications." *Criminology* 23:451–501.

Graham, Dorcas
  1976 "NCS evaluation of errors in coverage and content (1/76–6/76)." Memorandum. Washington, DC: U.S. Bureau of the Census.

Groves, Robert M., and Robert L. Kahn
  1979 *Surveys by Telephone: A National Comparison with Personal Interviews*. New York: Academy Press.

International Association of Chiefs of Police
  1976 *IACP/UCR Audit/Evaluation Manual*. Gaithersburg, MD: IACP.

Klecka, William R., and Alfred J. Tuchfaraber, Jr.
  1978 "Random Digit Dialing: A Comparison to Personal Surveys." *Public Opinion Quarterly* 42:105–114.

LaVange, Lisa and Ralph Folsom
  1984 Preliminary Main Effects Model Results for the NCS Longitudinal Data. Research Triangle Park, NC: Research Triangle Institute.

Lehnen, Robert G., and Albert J. Reiss, Jr.
  1978 "Some Response Effects of the National Crime Survey." Proceedings on Section on Survey Research Methods. Washington, DC: American Statistical Association.
  1981 "Recommendations on the reporting of national crime survey data." Unpublished draft.

Lynch, James P.
  1983 "Changes in police organization and their effects on the divergence of the UCR and NCS trends." Paper presented at the American Society of Criminology, Denver, CO.

Martin, Elizabeth
  1983 "Procedural history of changes in NCS instruments, interviewing procedures and definition." Washington, DC: Bureau of Social Science Research.

McCleary, Richard, Barbara Bienstadt, and James Erven
  1982 "Uniform crime reports as organizational outcomes: Three time series experiments." *Social Problems* 29:361–367.

Motor Vehicle Manufacturers Association
  1981 *MVMA Motor Vehicle Facts & Figures*. Detroit, Michigan: Motor Vehicle Manufacturers Association of the United States. p. 36.

Murphy, Linda R., and Charles D. Cowan
  1976 "Effects of Bounding on Telescoping in the National Crime Survey," paper presented at Annual Meeting of the American Statistical Assocation, August 23, 1976.
Murphy, Linda R., and Richard W. Dodge
  1981 "The Baltimore Recall Study (1970)," *The National Crime Survey: Working Papers, Volume 1: Current and Historical Perspectives*, edited by Robert G. Lehnen and Wesley G. Skogan, pp. 16–21, Washington, D.C.: U.S. Bureau of Justice Statistics.
Nelson, J.F.
  1978 "Alternative measures of crime: A comparison of the Uniform Crime Report and the National Crime Survey in 26 American cities." Presented at the American Society of Criminology meeting in Dallas.
Newsweek Magazine
  1981 "The Plague of Violent Crime." *Newsweek Magazine* 46:2, March 23.
New York Times
  1981 Editorial on "The conflict of UCR–NCS statistics." *New York Times* IV:14:1, April 19.
O'Brien, Robert M.
  1985 *Crime and Victimization Data: Volume 4*, Law and Criminal Justice Series. Beverly Hills, CA: SAGE Publications.
Penick, Bettye K. Edison, and Maruice Owens (eds.)
  1976 *Surveying Crime. A Report of the Panel for the Evaluation of Crime Surveys*. Washington National Academy of Science.
Poggio, Eugene, et al.
  1983 *Study of the National Uniform Crime Reporting Program of the Federal Bureau of Investigation: Phase I Interim Report*. Cambridge, MA: Abt Associates.
Police Executive Research Forum (PERF)
  1981 *Survey of Police Operational and Administrative Practices, 1981*. Washington, DC: PERF.
Reiss, Albert
  1967 *Measurement of the Nature and Amount of Crime: Studies in Crime and Law Enforcement in Major Metropolitan Areas*. Vol. I: Field Surveys III. Washington, DC: Government Printing Office.
Reiss, Albert J., Jr.
  1970 *The Police and the Public*. New Haven, CT: Yale University Press.
  1982 "Victimization productivity in proxy interviews." New Haven, CT: Institute for Social and Policy Studies, Yale University.
Roman, Anthony M., and Gregory E. Sliwa
  1982a "Study of the impact of the increased use of the telephone in the NCS: Reply to the Comments of Robert Groves." Memorandum. Washington, DC: U.S. Department of Commerce, Bureau of the Census.
  1982b "Reply to the comments by David Cantor on the study of the impact of the increased use of the telephone in the NCS." Memorandum. Washington, DC: U.S. Department of Commerce, Bureau of the Census.
Singh, Rajendra P.
  1981 "NCS Redesign—Preliminary Optimum Cluster Size Study," Memoran-

dum for Gary M. Shapiro, Assistant Chief for Programs, Statistical Methods Division, Washington, D.C.: U.S. Bureau of the Census, June 18, 1981.

Skogan, Wesley G.
1974   "The Validity of Official Crime Statistics: An Empirical Investigation. *Social Science Quarterly* 55: 25–38.

Skogan, Wesley G., and Robert Lehnen
1981   *The National Crime Survey: Working Papers.* Volume 1. Washington, DC: U.S. Bureau of Justice Statistics.

Sykes, Richard J. and J.P. Clark
1980   "Deference in police-civilian encounters." *Police Behavior: A Sociological Perspective*, pp. 120–131 in Richard Lyndman (ed.), New York: Oxford University Press.

Taylor, Bruce
1989   *Redesign of the National Crime Survey: Special Report.* Washington, DC: Bureau of Justics Statistics.

Tuchfarber, Alfred J., Jr. and William R. Klecka
1976   *Random Digit Dialing: Lowering the Cost of Victimization Surveys.* Washington, DC: Police Foundation.

Turner, Anthony G.
1977   *An Experiment to Compare Three Interview Procedures in the National Crime Survey*, Report, Washington, D.C: U.S. Bureau of the Census, December.

Walker, Samuel
1977   *A Critical History of Police Reform.* Lexington, MA: Lexington Books.

Washington Post
1981   Editorial on "Two reports on violent crime in the U.S." *The Washington Post*, A:16:1:Eg, May 5.

Wiley, Mary G. and Terry Hudik
1980   "Police citizen encounters: A field test of exchange theory." In Richard Lundman (ed.), *Police Behavior: A Sociological Perspective.* New York: Oxford University Press.

Woltman, Henry F.
1981   "Reference Period Resarch in the NCS," Memorandum for Gary M. Shapiro, Asst. Chief for Programs, Statistical Methods Division, Washington, D.C.: U.S. Bureau of the Census, May 26, 1981.

Woltman, Henry F., and John M. Bushery
1975   "A Panel Bias Study in the National Crime Survey," Paper presented at Annual Meeting of the American Statistical Association, Washington, D.C.: August 25, 1975.
1977   "Results of the NCS maximum personal visit-maximum telephone interview experiment." Memorandum. Washington, DC: Bureau of the Census.

Index

Research in Criminology

continued

Multiple Problem Youth:
Delinquency, Substance Use, and Mental Health Problems
D.S. Elliott, D. Huizinga and S. Menard

Selective Incapacitation and the Serious Offender:
A Longitudinal Study of Criminal Career Patterns
Rudy A. Haapanen

Deterrence and Juvenile Crime: Results from a National Policy
Experiment
Anne L. Schneider

Understanding Crime Incidence Statistics:
Why the UCR Diverges From the NCS
Albert D. Biderman and James P. Lynch

Developments in Crime and Crime Control Research: German Studies
on Victims Offenders and the Public
Klaus Sessar and Hans-Jürgen Kerner (Eds.)

Human Development and Criminal Behavior: News Ways of
Advancing Knowledge
Michael Tonry, Lloyd E. Ohlin, and David P. Farrington, with
contributions by Kenneth Adams, Felton Earls, David C. Rowe,
Robert J. Sampson, and Richard E. Tremblay

Urban Crime, Criminals, and Victims: The Swedish Experience
in an Anglo-American Comparative Perspective
Per-Olof Wikström